phases

globalization

Jürgen Osterhammel
and
Niels P. Petersson

Translated by Dona Geyer

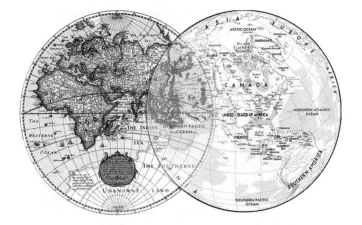

globalization
a short history

PRINCETON UNIVERSITY PRESS

PRINCETON AND OXFORD

First published in Germany under the title *Geschichte der Globalisierung.*
Dimensionen, Prozesse, Epochen

© Verlag C. H. Beck ohG, München 2003

English translation © 2005 by Princeton University Press
41 William Street, Princeton, New Jersey 08540

In the United Kingdom: Princeton University Press, 3 Market Place,
Woodstock, Oxfordshire OX20 1SY

Library of Congress Cataloging-in-Publication Data
Osterhammel, Jürgen.
[Geschichte der Globalisierung. English]
Globalization : a short history / Jürgen Osterhammel, Niels P. Petersson ;
translated by Dona Geyer.
p. cm.
Translation of: Geschichte der Globalisierung.
Includes bibliographical references and index.
ISBN 0-691-12165-6 (cloth : alk. paper)
1. Globalization—History. I. Petersson, Niels P. II. Title.
JZ1318.O8713 2005
303.48′2′09—dc22 2004058633

British Library Cataloging-in-Publication Data is available

Printed on acid-free paper. ∞

pup.princeton.edu

Printed in the United States of America

11 13 15 17 19 20 18 16 14 12

ISBN-13: 978-0-691-12165-9 (cl.)
ISBN-10: 0-691-12165-6 (cl.)
ISBN-13: 978-0-691-13395-9 (pbk.)

Contents

Preface   vii

I. "Globalization": Circumnavigating a Term   1
A Diagnosis of the Present and a Term
for a Historical Process   1
The Core Concept and the Controversies   5

II. The Dimensions of Globalization   13
World System—Imperialism—Global History   14
Networks and Interaction Spheres   21
Historical Periods   27

**III. The Development and Establishment of
Worldwide Connections Until 1750   31**
Long-distance Trade, Empires, Ecumenes   31
Gunpowder Empires and Maritime Domains   42
Holes in the Net   49

**IV. 1750–1880: Imperialism, Industrialization,
and Free Trade   57**
Early World Politics and Atlantic Revolutions   57
The Far-reaching Impact of the
Industrial Revolution   62
Empires and Nation-States   69
The Emergence of a World Economy   76

V. 1880–1945: Global Capitalism and Global Crises   81

The Experience of Globality, Global Economy,
and World Politics at the Turn of the Century   81
Imperialism and World War   90
1918–1945: Global Crises and Conflicts   99
The "American Century"   107

VI. 1945 to the Mid-1970s: Globalization Split in Two   113

Political Spaces: Power Blocs, Nation-States,
and Transnational Movements   113
The Institutions of the Global Economy   121
Sociocultural Globalization?   130

VII. Conclusion   141

A New Millennium   141
On the Road to a Global Age?   145
Globalization: Putting the Concept
into Perspective   150

Notes   153

Recommended Literature   171

Index   181

Preface

This book is the contribution of two historians to an ever-widening debate about globalization. Few subjects are more important for understanding the contemporary world, and few are more contested and more in need of careful empirical investigation. The debate on globalization takes place in many different fields and academic disciplines. Economics, sociology, political science, and cultural studies are only the most important among them. What historians have to offer is close attention to change. When they look at the world in the early twenty-first century, they ask how our present condition came about. They are interested in the emergence of the present, in historical parallels and precedents, and in possible alternatives and paths not taken.

Change can be described along various temporal scales, ranging from instantaneous events to long-term developments spanning centuries or even millennia. The word "globalization" indicates change and dynamism over time. It refers to a process or, as we will try to show, to a bundle of related processes that do not necessarily progress at the same speed or move in the same direction. Moreover, they affect the various parts of the world in quite different ways. When did globalization begin? The world did not turn "global" overnight. No single event, neither the invention of the Internet nor the fall of the iron curtain, inaugurated an entirely new age out of the blue. Globality has a history reaching back far before modern times. This book traces the emergence of relations between communities across vast spaces and long distances over the past seven or eight centuries. It grows more detailed as globalizing tendencies intensify in the more recent past. We do not deny that already in early ages travelers and traders performed feats of voyaging and land-bound transport. It is also obvious that several major civilizations, for example, China or the early the Arab-Muslim civilization, had good reasons to regard themselves as centers of the "world" as it was known to them. Yet we detect incipient globalization not before the epoch that, in Western terms, is known as the High Middle Ages. The Mongol world-empire of the thirteenth century, originating in Inner Asia, for the first time opened up the chance to spread goods and ideas across a huge space from the Yellow Sea to present-day Poland. It connected Latin and Orthodox Christendom, the Islamic world, and China in an unprecedented way.

"Globalization" implies more than just the existence of relations between distant places on earth. The term should only be used where such relations acquire a certain degree of regularity and stability and where they affect more than tiny numbers of people. Relations have to crystallize into institutions in order to gain permanence. The Mongolian empire was fragile and disintegrated after a few decades. Nowhere did it create a durable political order. This transience was different from the new empires of the sixteenth century. European overseas expansion resulted in large-scale colonization and state-building in the New

World and in the emergence of the Atlantic as a new arena of trade—in goods and enslaved people—between many different civilizations. At the same time, mighty continental empires were established or consolidated by indigenous rulers across Asia, while Europeans entered Asia as merchants and missionaries. Their early trading empires later grew into territorial dominion in India, Indonesia, and elsewhere.

However, the early history of globalization is not merely about imperial expansion. It is also about the emergence and growth of a world economy. The various empires slowly became enmeshed into even more extended webs of exchange. While long-distance trade by land and by sea is an ancient phenomenon, integrated world markets for goods, capital, and labor were unknown before the middle of the nineteenth century. Since that time, their evolution and their impact on individual countries and societies has been one of the major factors forging links across the planet. Yet another important aspect of globalization is an outlook that seeks to transcend parochialism and ethnocentrism, in other words, a "global consciousness." Even today, few people "think globally," and even fewer did so in the past. However, these cosmopolitan minorities who ~~start—~~ did possess a global perspective, for example, the early Jesuit missionaries or the philosophers and scientists of the Enlightenment, were pioneers who grappled with the tension between universal values and the plurality of cultures on earth. Such a tension is still very much with us.

The chapters in this book are arranged in chronological sequence. We distinguish between four major periods. Until the mid-eighteenth century, empire-building, trade, and religious solidarity encouraged intercontinental exchange on an expanding scale. From about the 1750s onward, political revolution in the Americas and in Europe intensified imperial rivalry, and the industrialization of some parts of the Northern Hemisphere created networks of traffic, communication, migration, and commerce that in density and strength surpassed anything known up to that time. Our third period begins in the 1880s and lasts until the end of World War II. Its main features were the politicization of globalization through attempts to turn it into an instrument of national policies; the seemingly final division of the world among the imperialist great powers; and the growth of global flows of capital and the rise of programs envisaging the reordering of the entire globe in terms of liberalism (Woodrow Wilson) or revolutionary socialism (Lenin). The 1930s and early 1940s witnessed a catastrophic breakdown of globalization. Characteristically, however, the crises and conflicts of those years were of a truly worldwide scope. The fourth period, beginning in 1945, was dominated by attempts to avoid the mistakes made during the period between the two world wars. While the world economy was reconstructed along liberal lines, the antagonism of the American-led "free world" and the Soviet bloc during the Cold War prevented many potential relations and linkages from unfolding. This is why we speak of "globalization split in two." During this fourth period, mass tourism, the rise of global media and global forms of entertainment, and the universal spread of Western patterns of consumption were already pointing toward the kind of everyday experience characteristic of the early twenty-first century. Problems such as environmental damage, competition over scarce resources (oil, for example), and even terrorism began to assume a transcontinental character. By the early 1980s many of the elements of contemporary globalization were in place.

This book is very short. The format allows us to develop our historical arguments as concisely as possible. At each stage we provide examples without trying to be exhaustive. Encyclopedic completeness cannot possibly be a goal of an interpretive and introductory text. A list of Recommended Literature will direct readers to a universe of historical detail. If this were a brief history of the world as a whole, the authors would have an obligation to deal evenhandedly with all civilizations and all parts of the planet. In a history of globalization, by contrast, we are free to choose where to place our emphasis. To give just one example, in writing about the later nineteenth century, it would simply be wrong not to be "Eurocentric." For other, both earlier and later, periods of history such a Eurocentric perspective is quite misguided.

The original German edition benefited from an interdisciplinary seminar, jointly taught with Aleida Assmann, S. N. Eisenstadt, and Bernhard Giesen at the University of Konstanz in summer 2003. For his support in bringing about an American edition we are greatly indebted to Sven Beckert. Jürgen Osterhammel also wishes to express his gratitude to the Netherlands Institute for Advanced Study (NIAS) and its former rector, H. L. Wesseling, for the opportunity to read and reflect leisurely on a boundless topic.

globalization

"Globalization":
Circumnavigating a Term

A Diagnosis of the Present and a Term
for a Historical Process

"Globalization" is a term often used to explain today's world. For years, it lay nearly dormant, used only in a few select publications by a handful of economists writing on very specialized topics. Then, in the 1990s, globalization was embraced by a wider public and has since skyrocketed to terminological stardom. It has been integrated into the vocabulary of numerous languages, and various scholarly fields have adopted it as a leitmotiv and the central category of their research. Every day the list of literature on globalization or globality, global history or global capitalism grows longer. The semantic thicket is already so dense that we need help in blazing a trail through it.[1] In addition to the studies examining the specific effects of current economic globalization, an increasing number of publications deal with this topic in a more general or theoretical nature. When journalists begin to philosophize about the state of affairs in the world, it does not take long before globalization is mentioned. The term is therefore in danger of becoming just another word generously used in the art of terminological name-dropping, a term whose exact meaning is irrelevant as long as it creates an impression of profundity strong enough to ward off skeptical questions. The general popularity of "globalization" is, however, more than just a symptom of a collective unwillingness to think. The term is unrivaled in its ability to fulfill a legitimate need: to give us a name for the times in which we live. In recent decades it has not been easy to succinctly express the nature of the contemporary era. In the 1950s many raved about the "atomic age." In the 1960s and 1970s some talked about advanced "industrial society" and others about "late capitalism." In the 1980s the term "risk society" got a good deal of attention and the "postmodern" came into fashion, but the latter could not gain a strong foothold in the consciousness of the general public because it seemed so intangible. "Globalization" is of an entirely different caliber. In a single word, this term summarizes a wide spectrum of experiences shared by many people. For one, the people of the world's wealthy nations find (nearly) the entire world at their doorstep every day thanks to modern forms of consumption and communication. For another, the breakup of the isolated world of the Soviet bloc appears to have left the planet as a whole permeated by uniform principles of modern Western lifestyles. Seen from an economic perspective, the liberation of market forces from governmental regulation and the technological innovation in the areas of data processing and communication seem to have helped create markets in which supply and demand can become effective worldwide. As wide as the gap may be between the extreme opaqueness shrouding the interdependencies of the global economy and the clarity with which daily experience demonstrates the growing irrelevance of borders, the term globalization has the significant advantage of doing justice to both sides, of reconciling reason and emotion and finding their common denominator. At the heart of this term is a dichotomy that proves time and again to be as trivial as it is true: the world is becoming noticeably "smaller" as distant lands are being linked ever more closely together. At the same time, the world is becoming "larger" because our horizons have never been so broad.[2] Therefore, whoever seeks to sum up "in a word" the zeitgeist of this most recent turn of the century finds little alternative but to resort to the constantly repeated assurance that we have entered the era of globalization.

This is the point where historians feel the need to intervene in the debate. Some of what is being presented in sociological literature as new findings seems already very familiar to them. Long before the word "globalization" came into being, for example, economic historians had rather precisely described the process of emergence and continued integration of a global economy. In their work, historians strive for precision both in the factual account and the ascription of cause and effect. Although historians, when in doubt, have preferred to support well-founded evidence over flashy arguments, they are just as susceptible to grand generalizations as are their colleagues in other disciplines. For quite a while now, historiography has explained the changes that the world has experienced in the last two and a half centuries with the help of all-encompassing concepts of historical processes, which—like their cousins, the famous "isms" (liberalism, socialism, etc.)—could be described as the "izations": rationalization, industrialization, urbanization, bureaucratization, democratization, individualization, secularization, alphabetization, to name a few. Although these processes each follow their own time pattern and are linked to one another in a very complicated way, what they all have in common is that they take place over a (very) long stretch of time, occur in various forms and intensities on all continents, and unleash a force of change seldom found in earlier, premodern history. The metaconcept of "modernization" attempts to integrate these various processes into a single, all-encompassing development.

Simply by virtue of the term's semantics, "globalization" seems predestined to qualify for a place among the macroprocesses of the modern world. We need not immediately endow the term with an importance that would place it directly next to (or even above) "modernization," nor must we see globalization as the main feature of global development in an increasingly complex set of distant contexts. It is enough just to ask whether "globalization" could possibly be as expressive and important a concept as, for example, "industrialization." That alone would be a remarkable achievement and would greatly enrich the interpretative repertoire of historiography. Such a concept would be even more welcome since none of the abovementioned "izations" conceptualizes links between peoples, states, and civilizations. They manifest themselves within national and regional frameworks and therefore are analyzed within these contexts. Should "globalization" earn a place among the major concepts of human development, the term would thus fulfill a huge need. It would be in a position to offer sanctuary to all those intercontinental, international, and intercultural notions that currently wander like homeless vagabonds amid our well-established historical "discourses."

The fact that such a need does indeed exist presents us with the stepping stone to the following discussion. Let it be clearly understood that we are not suggesting the wholesale dismissal of all previous historiography, and we are careful not to make the absurd claim to want to rewrite the history of the modern era as one of globalization. Instead, we will attempt to throw a new light on the past from the perspective of globalization. In other words, it is a truism that many aspects of our existence today can only be understood in connection with worldwide integration. Yet, have not integrative developments played a greater role in the past than is expressed in the current historiography? What sort of integrative developments were these? How did they function? Did they really add up to a singular process that justifies using the newly created term "globalization"? If so, can we then identify a point near the end of the twentieth century when the trends toward globalization became so dramatic and dominant that we dare to speak of a turning point, of the beginning of a new epoch, of a "global age" (Martin Albrow) or a "second modernity" (Ulrich Beck, Anthony Giddens) or any other label we might choose?[3]

The Core Concept and the Controversies

In the majority of the proposed definitions of "globalization," the factors that play a major role are the expansion, concentration, and acceleration of worldwide relations.

Definitions often also contain various diagnoses of our present era. Inherent in them is often the question of whether globalization means the demise of the nation-state, whether it will usher in cultural homogeneity throughout the world, or whether it will bestow new meaning on the concepts of time and space. All too often, such discussions on the *meaning* of globalization contain stark value judgments. On either end of the broad spectrum of opinion are the positions held by globalization enthusiasts and opponents, respectively. Whereas the former welcome globalization as the beginning of a new era of growth and prosperity, the latter see it as the emergence of global domination by big businesses originating from Western countries to the detriment of democracy, labor rights, poor countries, and the global ecological system.

If any consensus exists among authors of the various persuasions, then it is the assumption that globalization challenges the importance of the nation-state and alters the balance of power between states and markets in favor of the latter.[4] It is argued that those profiting from this development and from the steps taken by national governments to facilitate free trade are the multinational corporations, which can pick the least expensive locations for direct investment worldwide without being hampered by loyalty to their countries of origin. The ability of national governments to influence economic development and their access to resources, especially to taxes, is said to be impaired. The provisions of the welfare state are also being dismantled, thereby diminishing the legitimacy of the state—a development that in the eyes of neoliberal globalization enthusiasts means a gain of personal freedom, whereas for globalization opponents it is the onset of anarchy, which benefits only the strong. Thus, one of the central themes of social science today is the erosion of the (nation) state's external sovereignty, its domestic monopoly of force, and its ability to govern.[5]

There is also general agreement about a second characteristic of globalization, namely, its influence on everything covered by the rubric of "culture."[6] Cultural globalization, driven by communication technology and the worldwide marketing of Western cultural industries, was understood at first as a process of homogenization, as the global domination of American mass culture at the expense of traditional diversity. However, a contrasting trend soon became evident in the emergence of movements protesting against globalization and giving new momentum to the defense of local uniqueness, individuality, and identity. These movements used the same new technologies to pursue their own goals more efficiently and to appeal for support from world opinion. Roland Robertson has called this concurrent development of homogenization and heterogenization a simultaneous "universalization of particularism and the particularization of universalism." At the same time, he introduces the term "glocalization" in order to emphasize that global trends always have an impact on local communities and require special "absorption."[7] The outcome of cultural change through globalization is also often interpreted as "hybridity," meaning the result of new cultural elements being creatively adapted to mesh with existing ones.[8] Mass media, long-distance travel, and the global demand for certain consumer goods are considered to be the most important mechanisms of "glocalization."

In light of the ease and frequency with which people, goods, and especially information overcome great distances, numerous authors have described globalization as a fundamental change of the categories of time and space. The geographer David Harvey calls this "space-time-compression."[9] This can be considered as the third basic feature of a social scientific understanding of globalization. "Space-time-compression," starting with the radical reduction in telephone fees and the extensive use of electronic mail, creates a shared immediacy and a "virtual" togetherness and thereby produces the prerequisites for worldwide social relations, networks, and systems, within which effective distance is considerably smaller than geographical distance. The most important cause of this phenomenon is the increased speed of communication.

Another way to express this idea is to refer to "deterritorialization" or "supraterritoriality."[10] Location, distance, and borders no longer play a role in many social relationships. Scholars also tend to agree that globalization should not be understood as the intensified interaction between nationally delimited societies, but as a trend toward dismantling territoriality and dissolving spatially linked sovereignty—this being the geographic counterpart to interpretations emphasizing the retreat of the state in favor of self-regulating market forces.

Various leading participants in the debate on globalization use such a fundamental and widely accepted definition on which to base their more elaborately developed interpretations and prognoses. Of these, two should be mentioned: Martin Albrow's concept of "globality" and Manuel Castells's idea of "network society." For Albrow, "globality" turns the present into an era unlike anything else in history. The dimensions of globality, he argues, are reflected in the fact that environmental issues exist within the framework of a global ecological system; that the danger of global destruction is inherent in weapons of mass destruction; that communication systems and markets span the entire globe; and finally that globality has become reflexive, meaning that a growing number of people refer to knowledge about the global context of their actions and attitudes. Manuel Castells describes globalization as the emergence of a "network society," a social form he claims is also historically unprecedented. Computer technology has made it possible for the first time to organize flexible social relations independent of territories. In the information age, economics and politics are no longer organized in a big, hierarchical, bureaucratic way, but as loosely structured, horizontal networks. Thus, the basis for exercising power and distributing resources has changed. Power is no longer manifested in command and obedience but is anchored in the existence of a network organization set up each time for a specific purpose. In place of the dichotomies of repression and exploitation, the social categories "top" and "bottom," and geographic "centers" and "peripheries," the determining principle is whether one belongs to or is excluded from the network. The major fault line in Castells's new world divides those who are connected from those who are not.

In addition to such ambitious interpretations of at times prophetic caliber, there are more modest approaches in which globalization is not mystified into a historically effective force itself[11] but remains more of a descriptive, overarching concept for a series of concrete processes of transformation. For David Held and his coauthors, globalization appears as the result of processes that have been evolving, though not necessarily continuously, for a long period. Economic, political, cultural, and military complexes each continue to follow their own dynamics, and their respective scopes need not be overlapping. The impact of these processes differs depending on place, time, and social class. In this view, globalization is an open (i.e., not predetermined) process that substantially transforms (but does not eradicate) such institutions of human collective organization as states, companies, churches, and families. Unrelentingly it produces counterforces of fragmentation. James N. Rosenau and Ian Clark, two historically interested representatives of international relations theory, develop similar ideas. These so-called 'transformationalists' see globalization as a phenomenon of recent history, but one based on long-existing processes of spatially extensive political, economic, cultural, and military interaction.

Finally, it is certainly not hard to find skeptics of the globalization idea. They should not be confused with the at times very militant opponents of globalization. The latter share with their adversaries, the apostles of globalization, the belief that they are witnessing a fundamental transformation of the modern social and political world. Skeptics, however, see this belief as an exaggeration of reality; at times they even consider all the talk about globalization to be no more than an ideological cover-up for American strategies of economic control, while others suspect it is a propaganda trick of neoliberal business elites

and technocrats. Paul Hirst and Grahame Thompson see
the standard globalization literature as little more than a
collection of anecdotes, impressions, and individual facts
taken out of context and arranged to suggest that, taken
together, they constitute the "phenomenon" of globalization. Hirst and Thompson, who concentrate on the
economic aspects, do not find any such connection linking the numerous examples.

This points once again to the importance of terminol-
ogy. On the one hand, anyone who identifies the signs of
globalization as a functioning world market, free world
trade and the unimpaired movement of capital, migratory
movements, multinational corporations, an international
division of labor, and a world currency system will be able
to find globalization in the second half of the nineteenth
century. On the other hand, anyone searching for comprehensive worldwide networking "in real time" will, depending on their inclination, either feel they are witnessing the
dawning of a new era or indignantly refuse to accept such
a superficial diagnosis as the newest "master narrative" of
sociology. As historians, we would therefore be naïve to
ask "when globalization began" or "whether globalization
existed in the eighteenth century." The first thing we need
to do is establish our own concept of "globalization," one
that avoids both pedantry and excessive vagueness. Such
a concept must act like a searchlight to illuminate the past
without throwing the shadows of foregone conclusions
over what we will find.

The Dimensions
of Globalization

If globalization has emerged only in recent decades and
may even represent the beginning of a new historical
epoch, then it becomes necessary first to compare those
aspects that are new to those that existed previously.
However, if globalization results from the interaction
and mutual strengthening of long-term processes, then
we will find ourselves truly in the middle of important
problems of historical analysis. At first glance, it appears
as if historians have paid little attention to globalization
so far; the word "globalization" or even the adjective
"global" appears in the title of only a small number of
history books. This alone means little. Still, could one
of the most momentous processes of the modern era
have occurred secretly and unnoticed? Of course not. In
order to find all the pertinent literature, we must use
other keywords and rubrics. This in itself is one good reason to dissect the rather grandiose term of "globalization" into its various components and aspects, which is
the purpose of the second section of this chapter. However, the term "globalization" first needs to be placed
briefly within the context of the history of ideas and the
social sciences.

World System—Imperialism—Global History

Despite the universalism of its precursors and founders (from Montesquieu to Max Weber) who covered a spectrum of numerous civilizations, sociology had long been accustomed to studying societies in a strictly national framework—German, French, Japanese, and so on—as if societies could be neatly extracted from larger contexts. To a great extent, criticism of this approach went unheeded.[1] But as globalization became a popular catchword, people other than the specialists began to pay more attention to phenomena such as migration, worldwide communication, and global economic integration. The idea of society as a self-contained, coherent, and clearly demarcated entity—the "container theory" of society (Ulrich Beck)[2]— was called into question. New debates about nations and nationalism led to reconsiderations of the concept of the nation-state. The concept is not really appropriate for the early modern period nor for earlier epochs; even its pertinence for the early twenty-first century seems to be limited.

The shift in outlook took place more slowly among historians, the large majority of whom, as a rule, were and still are national historians, experts on the history of their own countries. Nevertheless, certain fields of study have produced findings that are useful for the history of globalization:

1. The history of "world economy," mainly that of international trade, was for a long time a focal point of research in economics, economic history, and economic geography. During the last two or three

decades, this field temporarily lingered in the
shadows and is only now beginning to experience
a revival of interest. The renewed thrust of European
colonial expansion after 1880 and the simultaneous
processes of intensification in the international
movement of goods and capital were being com-
petently described by observers at that time. One
center for such research was the Institut für
Weltwirtschaft (Kiel Institute for World Economics),
founded in Kiel in 1914 and still in existence. The
analyses compiled both there and elsewhere are
valuable sources today for reconstructing global economic relations. A well-covered area of research,
particularly in Britain as the one-time center of
world finance, is the worldwide flow of capital and
the history of multinational corporations. Since the
1990s Anglo-American research has applied the
tools of economists to economic history (and the
insights of history to current debates in economics)
to study global economic connections with increasing intensity. At first, attention focused on the clas-
sical themes of trade and capital transfers but soon
broadened to include other subjects like migration,
labor markets, agriculture, and the role of institutions such as the various international monetary
systems since the mid-nineteenth century. This
work is beginning to provide an overview of the
evolution of global factor markets. It allows us to
break down the catchall notion of "economic globalization" into more specific components and types.
Furthermore, it emphasizes the importance of the

mid-nineteenth century as a watershed between the period when mostly "noncompeting goods" were exchanged between continents and the period when markets for widely used commodities—especially foodstuffs—and for labor became globally integrated. This research also suggests that the aspects of migration and of national and international institutions are at least as important to economic globalization as those of trade and investment.[3]

2. Migration research, which has also existed since the late nineteenth century, combines the questions and methods of demography and social history. It attempts to record migratory movements statistically and geographically, seeks to discover the motives and reasons for emigration (without excluding cases of forced abduction and expulsion), and examines the experiences of immigrants in their new environment.[4] One of its major topics is long-distance, transoceanic migration. If migrant communities maintain contact with their native countries over longer periods of time, we speak of "diasporas."[5] They are a prime example of social discontinuity in space. Impressive findings have resulted from research on the history of diasporas throughout the world, such as the Chinese communities in Southeast Asia, North America, the Caribbean, and Europe. One well-established field featuring an unusually broad variety of approaches and methods is the study of the Atlantic slave trade and of New World slavery.[6] The best historical writing on slavery demonstrates how to combine global perspectives

with attention to local conditions and even individual biographies.

3. The history of international relations (including military history) has so far usually been a history either of bilateral relations between countries or of internal developments within the European system of great powers. For a long time, even the world wars of the twentieth century were not analyzed to the full extent within the global context in which they occurred. Meanwhile, the number of books in which the authors examine systemic relations that transcend continental borders is increasing.[7] International history and international relations theory have broadened not only their geographical but also their conceptual horizons. Increasingly, theorists of international relations are taking into account the actors found at levels above, below, and alongside the nation-state, while historians of international relations see their subject as inseparable from cultural and social developments that they would have left to historians of other subfields to study not long ago. Indeed, it can be argued that this is the only way to adequately assess the continuously changing place and role of the nation-state, the chief actor in international politics. Thus, more and more global processes, connections, and structures come within the purview of international history, including information and cultural networks, transnational political activism, and international organizations and regimes.[8]

4. The history of imperialism and colonialism is a particularly important cornerstone for the history of

globalization. It is not by accident that several of the leading international representatives of this field propagate an expansion of "imperial history" into "global history."[9] For a long time, work in this field concentrated on the colonial history of the researcher's own country. However, in the last two decades, it has branched out to include a multitude of new topics and now more closely approximates an *histoire totale* than do other special fields in history. It adopts impulses from ethnology (specifically, cultural anthropology) and profits from the work being done in the neighboring "postcolonial studies" on issues of cultural identity-building—often cases of "glocalization"—as well as from its criticism of Eurocentrism. Three recent trends are particularly important. Firstly, the old concept of "empire" is being revitalized. Whereas "imperialism" is usually taken to refer to the expansionist policies of modern great powers, "empire" denotes large-scale structures of domination from the beginning of organized statehood to the present time.[10] A great challenge is the search for similarities and differences between the seaborne empires created by western Europeans in the early and late modern periods and the continuous, continental empires to be found all over Eurasia from China to the Habsburg domain. Secondly, the "new colonial history" sees colonies as multiethnic spheres where a permanent process of negotiation and identity formation takes place among the various groups of colonizers and the colonized.[11] Thirdly, the famous question about the imperial "impact" on subjugated countries and civilizations is being reversed and turned into an inquiry into the repercussions and backlashes that colonialism caused in the metropoles.

None of these four fields can be identified with a single "grand" theory of global change. Do such comprehensive approaches even exist? Parallel to the emergence and growing popularity of the topic of "globalization" in the social sciences since the early 1990s, there has also been a great interest shown in "world history" or "global history," particularly in the English-speaking world.[12] In his authoritative compendium on global approaches to history, Patrick Manning suggests that the term "world history" be adopted everywhere and defined as "the study of connections between communities and between communities and their environments."[13] Without being pedantic, we prefer to retain a distinction between "world history" and "global history" as two equally legitimate yet different modes of thought.[14] "World history" is the history of the various civilizations, especially their internal dynamics, and a comparison of them, whereas "global history" is the history of contacts and interactions between these civilizations. Global history is neither an independent field of research with characteristic methods nor a dogma with regard to its themes and questions. It mistrusts, for example, trivial assumptions such as those assuring us that the world is increasingly becoming a "global village," and it rejects the idea that modern history has already been exhaustively described as the "rise of the West."[15] We can view global history as a type of "diagonal" inquiry cutting across national histories and as an attempt to analyze relations among peoples, countries, and civilizations from perspectives other than those of power politics and economics.[16] Global history includes the history of globalization, but it can also study relations that do not directly contribute to globalization.

Anyone determined to find an all-encompassing conceptual framework will inevitably come across the term "world-system." In a long series of influential publications appearing since the early 1970s, the American sociologist Immanuel Wallerstein has developed a theory of the "modern world-system," a theory that has been judged a significant achievement even by its critics. Wallerstein bases his work on historical research and, so far, has applied his theory to the period from about 1500 to 1850.[17] This means that his world-system analysis has not yet taken up the challenge of describing truly global connections, making the theory to date an interpretation of the expansion of the "capitalist global economy" as it originated in Europe. Wallerstein has not yet even reached the point at which the United States intervenes to shape economic relations worldwide. However, many have been inspired by his ideas and have often applied them in very productive ways to many topics.

Several elements of Wallerstein's analytical method have proven effective outside the rather rigid confines of his theoretical framework. Three of these should be mentioned in particular. The first is a scale of levels of inquiry that ranges from the world system down to the private household and does not focus much on the nation-state. The second is the concept of an "incorporation" of external areas on the periphery of a continuously expanding capitalist world economy. This process of incorporation can be precisely described case by case in geographical and institutional terms and can be differentiated by degree.[18] The third is the term "semi-periphery," meaning a variable third position located between the economic "centers" and the peripheries.[19] Wallerstein argues that the "modern world-system" is encompassed by an "outer arena" that is not yet incorporated into the system, something like a geographical equivalent of the "precapitalist mode of production" that, over time, is swallowed up by capitalism in the theory of Karl Marx. Since Wallerstein is not very interested in what actually happens in this "outer arena," he cannot be considered a "world historian" in the strictest sense. Still, this theory reminds us that connections do not only "emerge" anonymously but are often created by strong and dynamic centers.

Networks and Interaction Spheres

Is there a way to approach the (pre)history of globalization that enables us to study more than just the unrelated parallel histories of individual civilizations and countries without requiring us to accept immediately the idea of the world-system (or the comparable creation emerging from sociology, the "world society")?[20] Is there no other perspective of the world than "from above"? Can we not also analyze it "from below"? This has already been done by a number of sociologists and ethnologists who have investigated networks of interactions. In their research, they discovered that even seemingly isolated village communities take part in long-range interaction in areas such as cultural-religious communication, money circulation, or marriage relations. At the same time, individuals even in such small groups participate in various overlapping though not congruent social contexts, which therefore cannot be seen as "components" of a spatially delimited societal "whole." Paradoxically, it thus appears to be more promising to begin the study of worldwide integration on the level of individual action, instead of focusing on the world as a whole.

Because we would like to approach globalization processes by studying interactions between individuals and groups, the concept of networks will be one of the most important ones used here.[21] Actually, this method is nothing new: economists in the early twentieth century were describing the world economy as a tightly interwoven global "network" that was especially dense in Europe. This network featured innumerable intertwined "threads" linking "each individual business operation, even the smallest and most modest . . . with millions of other businesses" so that the development of the "modern industrial and commercial states" could "only be understood and judged from the standpoint of a world economy."[22] Elementary network analysis does not take into consideration such complicated structures. Instead, it is necessary to emphasize that not every social transaction between more than two people should immediately be considered a network, just as not every coin that is found in an archeological excavation far from its place of origin must be proof of globalization. A network requires a certain degree of longevity and institutional reinforcement; yet even if it does have these, notes Manuel Castells, it remains a flexible but not very stable form of social organization. He argues that only with the advent of new information technology have we gained the means necessary to develop networks with the same stability as hierarchical organizations and thus to make them fundamental structures for economic and political life.[23] From a completely different starting point, namely, the theory of international relations, John W. Burton successfully developed in the early 1970s his "cobweb model" of social relations. For example, Burton suggested that all telephone conversations, travel, or movements of goods be entered on a map of the world without political borders. Burton's map depicts no territories and borders, only social interactions. The picture that emerges is similar to those of the "Earth by Night," obtained by superimposing satellite photos that show no borders but only areas of concentrated human settlement with a high degree of energy consumption. Only in this "world of transactions," as Burton calls it, do interactions grow into networks, structures, or systems.[24]

In other words, it is possible for interactions to transform themselves into networks. In turn, networks gain greater stability through institutions that are often the result of political will, such as a diplomatic alliance or an international trade agreement. The network concept does suffer from one disadvantage common to every effort to give social categories a spatial dimension, namely, that it tends to trivialize societal processes, to flatten hierarchies and power differences, and to overlook the varying depth and intensity of relationships.[25] The fact that networks cross or eliminate existing boundaries does not prevent them from creating new ones. This is an aspect in which Wallerstein's insistence on contradictions, conflicts, and center-periphery imbalances can have a correcting effect. Very seldom do interaction networks spread evenly around the world. They tend to be concentrated in what become interaction spheres, which are determined in part by the natural environment. Even if we no longer consider the nation-state our main point of reference, we will see that, for most of history, interaction and communication have not taken place on a global scale but within smaller spheres, the extension of which can be discerned but seldom clearly delimited. However, these spheres can be large enough to encompass entire continents and oceans. To a great extent, the history of globalization is about the emergence of such spheres from interactions and networks and about the connections that have grown between them.[26]

By speaking of networks, we do not mean to give the banal impression that everything is linked to everything else. Interactions have an organizing principle. Some of them actually do turn out to be reciprocal and interactive, such as bartering. Others do not. The Atlantic slave trade of the early modern period only flowed in one direction; very few of the kidnapped Africans ever returned to their homelands. Still, the slave trade was part of a tricontinental network referred to as "triangular trade." Commodity chains, meaning the sequence of all raw materials, intermediate goods, and services going into the creation of a certain finished product, appear at first glance to be linear in form. However, the interaction among a number of such chains creates spheres of economic interaction that encompass the entire world.[27] Such interaction spheres can be identified only if we draw up empirically supported balance sheets of integration—although, for the ages prior to the availability of statistics, we must make do with estimates.

Of the many recurring questions raised in connection with interactions, the two most prominent concern their range and their importance. It does indeed make a difference whether a country, like France, was not involved to any significant degree in the major European emigrations to America of the late nineteenth and early twentieth centuries or whether a country, like Ireland, lost a considerable portion of its population through emigration: in 1914, two-thirds of all Irish-born lived abroad.[28] Likewise, such population movements affected the United States, where large Irish "immigrant communities" emerged, but no French ones. (The latter did exist in Canada as a result of earlier immigration movements.) The criteria of range and importance also need to be interpreted in direct connection to one another. There have always been local networks, but in the course of globalization, the relative importance of networks with a wider and, in extreme cases, global range has increased. In other words, distant lands become increasingly important in the lives of certain groups of people. Around 1800, a product "made in China"—such as porcelain or silk—was without fail a luxury good for Europeans. Today it is a common commodity.

Integration also differs in intensity and speed of contact. In this regard, much depends on the technical means available and on organizational and institutional prerequisites that are always necessary to efficiently apply technology. We also need to look at the mediums of integration.

Even with quite minimal transportation capacities, the transfer of ideas or of metals vital as means of economic or military power can have a big impact over large distances. The intentional or accidental importation of infectious diseases, plants, or animals can create causal relations between societies without any direct contact between peoples.[29] In a certain sense, the "Americanization" of Germany did not begin in 1945 but rather in the eighteenth century, with the introduction of the potato.

These examples differ in two other important dimensions: the durability and frequency of interaction. By repeating the interaction at regular intervals, participants can create a tight network from what was at first merely a variety of interactions. Such a network would over time produce a stable division of labor among the participants and orient them to the economic needs and symbolic systems of their respective partners. In the various dimensions of social action, networks can develop their own expansion and dynamics. It is also possible that a strong political center manages to confine networks to a geographical space, or that they are "coordinated" by the dynamics of some overarching conflict.[30] Dynamics can freeze, and some processes can be reversed. We are often witnesses to the tearing apart, shrinking, and thinning out of relational networks and the weakening of the institutions that stabilize them. Deglobalization is not a vision for the future but a historically observable phenomenon.

If we conceive globalization as the development, concentration, and increasing importance of worldwide integration, then the concept loses its static character and its aspect of totality. The question is no longer whether the term "globalization" is an adequate description for the present state of the world. Instead, it directs attention to the history of worldwide integration, its development and erosion, its intensity and effects.

Historical Periods

Let us close by addressing the topic of periodization, meaning the division of historical developments into specific periods of time. There is no way to get around periodization in the telling of history. Historical processes seldom occur with any sort of mechanical regularity. They are subject to acceleration and deceleration. They are characterized by hiatuses and thrusts, by ebb and flow, and by conjunctures of rapid innovation. Only for the most important dates in political and military history—such as 1789, 1914, 1945, or 1989—do the demarcations between "eras" seem to be self-evident. However, even such spectacular upheavals do not inevitably represent concurrent turning points in those aspects of life that develop more continuously than political events do. Because globalization involves a variety of these aspects—business, technology, state organization, and culture, just to name the most important ones—the various periodizations overlap. This makes it particularly difficult to subdivide history in an unequivocal way. Yet, every reasonably justified proposal for periodization is worth debating. The following is our proposal.

We consider it problematic, on the one hand, to assume that globalization has been going on for thousands of years.[31] On the other hand, no one today can seriously contend that all premodern societies were small, compact units based solely on a self-sufficient economy within the framework of the household, the village, or at best a symbiosis between town and countryside. Throughout earlier periods of history, there were repeated attempts at globalization that always broke off at some point. Therefore, we can view these events as the prehistory of globalization. We agree with Immanuel Wallerstein insofar as we interpret a new globalization initiative that began around 1500 with the emergence of the Portuguese and Spanish colonial empires as the beginning of a basically irreversible process of worldwide integration. Exploration and regular trade relations put Europe, Africa, Asia, and America in direct contact for the first time. By the mid-1750s this contact had grown into a stable multilateral interdependency.

Therefore, by the mid-eighteenth century transcontinental networks had been established that were at least economically stable and potentially influential. What comes next, in the period we date from about 1750 to 1880, is an expansion of worldwide integration unprecedented in its intensity and influenced by the new capacities in production, transportation, and communication created by the Industrial Revolution. Politically, however, Europe retreats into itself in this period. The structures of colonial empire in America disappear except for a few insignificant remnants. The "emergence of the world economy" takes place under the conditions of predominant free trade. At the same time, European institutions, including the nation-state, and European or "Western" thought are being exported throughout the world. In the

1860s and 1870s we see certain economic spheres being affected for the first time by truly global interdependencies, several of which can be demonstrated statistically. After 1880 globalization begins to become politicized. By this time national societies want to rein in the effects of global economic integration. Outwardly, the global economy is perceived as world politics, as a function of national power. Soon conflicts arise among the "world powers" that herald an age of economic deglobalization, global crises, and world wars. When this period ends after 1945, a deliberate attempt is made to establish a better world order according to two competing models in two competing power blocs. Through this arrangement, structures are established within which globalization developed as we know it today—particularly through decolonization, multinational corporations, foreign aid policy, consumer society, and so on. At the same time, a new kind of globalization becomes increasingly prominent as people slowly perceive the world as a *Schicksalsgemeinschaft*, a community of fate threatened by nuclear annihilation and confronted with environmental problems that transcend national borders. The exact end of this age, which many have considered to be a golden age of the world economy, is an issue so controversial that we do not wish to make a definitive pronouncement here. Our analysis concludes in the 1970s. However, one thing is very clear: the collapse of the Soviet bloc in 1989–91 did not signify the sudden emergence of a thoroughly new world; rather, the collapse itself was for the most part the result of globalizing forces that were observed in the 1970s.

The Development and Establishment of Worldwide Connections Until 1750

Long-distance Trade, Empires, Ecumenes

Soon after Immanuel Wallerstein first outlined his historical theory that a "modern world-system" had emerged in the sixteenth century, the almost inevitable objection was raised that similar world systems had existed much earlier. According to some authors, such systems appeared as far back in history as five thousand years ago.[1] One of the motors driving this criticism was the political aim to discredit Wallerstein for his supposed "Eurocentrism." Indeed, Wallerstein does describe the "rise of the West," a history that leaves no doubt about the uniqueness of modern Europe. Even Wallerstein would not deny this. However, if others could convincingly argue that the world has repeatedly seen the rise and fall of world-systems throughout history, then it would be difficult to attribute such a special role to the modern history of the European-Atlantic realm.

We do not have to take a position in this rather quibbling debate in order to acknowledge that it has renewed academic interest in large-area integration in both the premodern and modern periods of history. Such integration took on various forms, of which three are particularly important. The first of these was the consolidation—usually coerced in the beginning—of smaller political units into an empire. With the creation of such empires, smaller political units such as kingdoms, tribal federations, or city states were swallowed up by a larger entity that was characterized by (a) a hierarchy of rule established for the entire empire, often with a monarch (emperor) at the top, (b) a military apparatus that could be deployed over vast areas, and (c) the symbolically underscored claim that the empire's center was the center of all known civilization. Even though this entity might also have been held together by some cultural "glue," an empire was basically an organization of centralized coercion and therefore never a "network." If ever the military arm of the empire became paralyzed, there was always the danger that individual regions would declare their independence from the empire and that border areas would be conquered by aggressive neighboring peoples.

A second form of integration was the religious ecumene.[2] Empire and ecumene could roughly overlap, although this is not what usually occurred. As a rule, the area in which a religion prevailed was far larger than that of the political and military entity that emerged in connection with the religion in question. Christianity, Islam, and Buddhism could not be contained within political borders. Only in China were the borders of its political geography nearly identical to those of religious geography. At least in times when the Chinese empire was strong, it was identical for the most part with that area in which the upper class followed the moral teachings of

Confucianism, which should not really be called a "religion." From here, Confucianism spread to neighboring countries such as Japan (without ever dominating the religious landscape), a land never ruled by the Chinese emperor. Consequently, an ecumene generally consisted of numerous political units. Their common religion did not always guarantee that they would peacefully coexist with one another, as both modern European history and the century-long tension between the Islamic lands of Iran and the Ottoman empire illustrate. In turn, an empire did not necessarily have to embrace a religion claiming universal validity; it might have what amounted to simply a number of local cults. The Mongolian empire of the thirteenth century, for example, existed without a "high" religion. However, this was one reason why the empire existed only for a relatively short period: its "ideological" cohesion was weak. Religious ecumenes would have remained very loosely organized had they only been based on a common set of spiritual beliefs. As it were, they became more than "imagined communities." Two components had to evolve in order to guarantee a stable unity: the gravitation toward holy centers, namely, pilgrimages (often over long distances), and the widespread commitment to certain rules governing ritualistic and daily life. In other words, people adhered as a matter of course to a catalog of duties that transcended geographical and even linguistic borders. One such example would be the set times of day that every believer in the Islamic world devotes to prayer. Often, but not always, religious ecumenes were also cemented by the study of holy scriptures such as the Bible or the Koran. What was anything but common was the existence of a centralized church organization featuring a clerical hierarchy that was, to a degree, independent of secular powers. This remains one of the characteristics unique to Roman Catholicism.

The third form of integration was long-distance trade. We hesitate to use the term "networks," although these certainly did exist. Still, various trade routes often established lasting connections between centers of civilizations far apart from one another. We see this in the silk trade between China and the Mediterranean region, the shipping routes between the Arabian peninsula and India, and the more frequently traveled caravan routes of the Near East and North Africa. Across such routes traveled people (often also slaves), goods and coins, artwork and ideas. Historians have only just begun to discover the diversity of such mobility in many parts of the world. Whereas it used to be thought that immobile peasant societies were the norm in the premodern world, today we are discovering that contact, transfer, and exchange occurred to a degree that can seldom be considered marginal. Even that era of transition from European antiquity to the Middle Ages (ca. 300–900 A.D.), an era so characterized by contraction and barbarism that it is often called the Dark Ages, has recently been presented as a new configuration of dynamic relations in communication and commerce.[3]

Lastly, we could even think of a fourth form of long-range integration: the mass migration of populations. The fields of archeology, ethnology, and historical genetics,[4] an area that has recently become particularly helpful to historians, are finding more and more evidence of migrations that cover sometimes as many as thousands of kilometers over land and sea. Well-known examples are the prehistoric settlement of America from northern Asia (starting perhaps about 70,000 B.C.); the colonization in the period between approximately 1500 and 800 B.C. of the eastern Pacific islands by the people of the Marquesas Islands, a highly mobile seafaring people; and the expansion eastward, westward, and southward of the Bantu-speaking peoples of the Niger-Congo region between 500 B.C. and 1000 A.D. Yet such migrations seldom led to permanent, far-reaching structures. The people left their original homeland, never returned, and maintained no or merely weak contact with anybody possibly left behind. Nor did the migrations take place on a regular basis, as did the Atlantic trade in African slaves during early modern history. All of these factors distinguish the early migration of peoples from those having taken place since the sixteenth century. Not until then did the history of migration begin under the portent of globalization.

When we attempt to review world history for approximately the thousand years preceding 1500—in what would be a very long definition of the Middle Ages—two thrusts in long-range integration stand out. If, for reasons of simplification, we use a schematic numbering of the centuries, we can date these thrusts from the eighth and thirteenth centuries. The most important development in the first phase was the emergence and military expansion of a new monotheistic religion on the periphery of the Arabian desert. Around 800, about two hundred years after the founding of Islam by the Prophet Muhammad, a gigantic area ranging from Andalusia in the west to Samarkand in present-day Uzbekistan was under the rule of a Muslim military aristocracy. Despite the political fragmentation in this region, which was bridged for only a few decades around 800 by something resembling a unified empire under the Abbasid caliphate with Baghdad as the capital, the cohesion of the new religious ecumene was extremely stable. With the exception of Spain, all of the Islamized areas from this period are still part of the *umma*, the community of Muslim believers. At about the same time, an empire was revived in East Asia, the contours of which are still recognizable today. The Chinese Tang dynasty resurrected the empire of the Han dynasty to about the same size it had been when it fell in 220 A.D. It stretched from the Yellow Sea to just before Tashkent in the west. Nearly all of the regions over which the Tang emperor claimed to rule belong today to the People's Republic of China.

What sort of a relationship existed between these two culturally different civilizations, both of which were at the same time the greatest centers of power of their age? The question is interesting insofar as these two civilizations were undergoing analogous and even synchronic development. Military conquest was followed in both cases by a flowering of urban culture and commerce.[5] Still, the contact between them was limited to a short military confrontation in central Asia in the 750s. Apart from the fact that the ancient Chinese invention of paper made its way over Samarkand and Baghdad to Europe, what little contact there was between the two did not have any transforming impact.[6] The most powerful military and economic centers on earth at the time remained self-contained.

The second major thrust of long-range integration to take place during the Middle Ages was not merely a replay of the first. Granted, the impetus came once again from the periphery in much the same way as Islam had emerged from the fringes of the Byzantine empire. Nearly six hundred years after the advent of Islam, a powerful army of nomadic horsemen burst forth from the steppe just north of the Chinese empire. United for the first time in 1206 under the leadership of Genghis Khan, within a short span of time these Mongol tribes pushed eastward as far as Korea, westward to the gates of Vienna and Damascus, and southward as far as the Indochinese peninsula. From the havoc wreaked by these military advances arose after 1259 something resembling a loose imperial federation, whose gradual decline did not begin until 1368, when the Mongols were run out of China.[7]

For good reason, the Mongols were not shown in a sympathetic light in the chronicles of their Christian, Chinese, and Arabian-Persian victims and adversaries. Historians today offer a more differentiated historical evaluation and emphasize the extraordinary freedom to travel and trade in Eurasia during the "Pax Mongolica." For the first time, European missionaries were able to make their way into East Asia, although their efforts to convert the population there met with no significant success. By widening our view to include the flourishing of long-distance trade within Western Europe, India, and Southeast Asia, as well as the Mediterranean expansionism of both the crusaders and the maritime republics, the picture of the thirteenth century that comes into sharper focus is one in which opportunity for migration and exchange expanded to an unprecedented level.[8] The increased mobility was also one significant cause for the spread of the bubonic plague, which originated in central Asia, reached the first large cities in China by about 1330, and made its way to Portugal, Morocco, and Yemen over the next twenty years. Hence, Eurasia was first united in calamity through an invasion of warriors on horseback and microbes.[9] Despite the far-reaching impact of the Mongolian empire, it did not contribute directly to the development of worldwide structures. The Mongols did indeed open up spaces and opportunities, but they themselves were at best parasitical in their treatment of the political and cultural institutions that they came across. There was hardly a case in which some sort of constructive impulse emanated from Mongolian rule, comparable to powers spearheading globalization later in the modern period.

The devastating Mongolian invasion was part of what made the Eurasian High Middle Ages so open, as were the universally oriented teachings and beliefs of theologians and philosophers in the Arabian, Latinized Christian, and Chinese worlds. This changed in the period from about the fourteenth to the sixteenth centuries, when this openness gave way to a strengthening of integrative tendencies *within* already existing units and an increasing demarcation *between* them. China had been the leading Asian sea power for four hundred years but lost this standing around 1430, at a time when the empire of the Ming dynasty became mired in a long, defensive war against the reinvigorated Mongols. For the next three hundred years, Chinese expansion was stopped in its tracks. China interacted with the outside world by way of an increasingly ritualized "tribute system" that symbolically confirmed time and again the position of the emperor as the sole ruler of the East and also maintained the status quo. It was only then that China turned into the isolated—although internally malleable—"Middle Kingdom" that Western observers became acquainted with in the seventeenth century. Japan, which always managed to remain independent of China, even went a step further. Once it was unified under one ruler around 1600, it reduced its participation in overseas trade in East Asia and refused to engage in any form of foreign politics until the mid-nineteenth century. For foreigners who were not Chinese, Korean, or part of a small contingent of closely monitored Dutch merchants, the archipelago was nearly inaccessible.[10]

Meanwhile, the regions of western and southern Eurasia were undergoing a contradictory development.[11] On the one hand, denominational schism and religious wars led to an internal crisis within the Christian ecumene, while on the other hand, the borders between the neighboring cultural realms of Christianity and Islam became more strongly demarcated than ever before. Muslims were expelled from Spain. In the Near East, the Ottoman Turks amassed great power and spread their control rapidly over the region, causing the downfall of the Byzantine empire and claiming its inheritance, geopolitically speaking. The center of the military conflict moved from the Levant, where it had been located during the Crusades, to the Balkans. Belgrade became the northernmost outpost of the Ottoman empire (and remained so until 1867). During this period of continual hostilities, the interest of Christians and Muslims in one another waned in comparison to what it had been in the thirteenth century. The two large religious ecumenes drew back from one another more than they had during the High Middle Ages. The gradually emerging field of oriental studies in Europe (for which the counterpart of "occidental studies" did not exist in the Islamic world) was not able to ease the atmosphere of religious and political hostility. Economically, however, the countries of Europe, the Near East, and the Middle East were much more open and accessible to the outside world than were China and Japan at the time. Much as during antiquity, the Mediterranean region and its neighboring areas were crisscrossed with trade routes that extended over the Alps, out to the Black Sea, and down into sub-Saharan Africa. Integration continued to advance through long-distance trade, which became increasingly vulnerable to the economic cycles affecting the entire Mediterranean region.

At the same time, the imperial mode of integration was revived. In the cultural spheres of both the Islamic and Christian worlds, a "universal monarchy" was no longer conceivable. Yet political fragmentation into tiny territorial realms was also avoided. Granted, central Europe, Italy, southern India, and Malaya did remain politically fragmented, although this was not always to the detriment of the people living there. Otherwise, large sovereignties were created. In the East, these were multiracial empires, founded by military aristocracies and led by powerful monarchs who had to prove themselves both as military leaders and civil organizers during the periods of conquest and state-building. The first of this type was the Ottoman empire, which appeared in its fully developed state around

1500. It was followed in the succeeding decades by the empire of the Safawid shahs in Iran and the Moghul empire in northern India. Also belonging to this category were the Muscovite empire, the nucleus of what later became the enormous continental empire of the Romanov czars, and in many respects the Habsburg dynasty, which ruled its empire from Vienna. This type of empire did not require an Islamic foundation or origin in order to flourish. Each of these empires created relatively uniform economic spheres and participated in long-distance trade beyond its borders. The demarcation of these borders was seldom very clear; at their edges, the empires conducted alliance diplomacy. Long-distance trade usually lay in the hands of minorities specializing in it (such as the Greeks, Armenians, and Parsees), who were granted protection by the empires in case they did not adhere to the official religion.

During this same period in western Europe, states were consolidating as a result not of conquest from outside but of the evolution of medieval monarchies. These differed from the multiracial empires in that they were religiously and ethnically homogeneous. England, France, and Spain represented best this type of "territorial state"; in the early eighteenth century the kingdom of Prussia also moved up into this class. One particularity of Europe was the new type of integration that resulted from the great crisis of the seventeenth century, known as the Thirty Years' War, in which the "system" of independent states made its own rules. Peace could not be forced upon a region by a warlord; it had to be created by consensus instead. But we must not overlook just how little the Peace of Westphalia of 1648 and the political order it established actually pacified the continent. In those lands where an imperial universal monarchy functioned—as in China—this was a better guarantee for domestic peace.

Gunpowder Empires and Maritime Domains

The political order established through the Peace of Westphalia was never thought to be more than a means to stabilize central and western Europe. It certainly was not intended to be a framework for world peace, and accordingly it did not include the overseas possessions of the European states. By about 1650, these possessions had reshaped the context of integration on earth to a considerable extent, and it was foreseeable that the conflicts fought between Europeans on the "periphery" would not be without direct consequences for Europe itself in the long run. Usually, the years 1450 to 1500 are said to represent a major turning point in history, the beginning of "modern history," no less. Recently, questions have been raised about the applicability of this periodization with regard to Europe; it definitely is not applicable for large parts of the world, such as East Asia. From the perspective of world history, though, it is valid for many reasons, including the following five.

First, we no longer attribute the same importance we once did to the exploratory journey of Vasco da Gama from Portugal around the Cape of Good Hope to India in 1498, because we know more about earlier economic contacts in and around the Indian Ocean and about the overland routes across all of East Asia. India was not "discovered" as quickly as America was, and the Europeans were not the first people to establish transoceanic travel routes. Still, it is correct and significant that within a few years after this journey, armed Portuguese ships had established a series of European footholds all along the maritime landscape from Mozambique to Malacca, for which there was no precedent. The Portuguese did not establish a territorial colonial empire and never ruled over large Asian populations, but they did manage to work their way into the local trading networks with their special form of militarized "crown capitalism" and to cover Asian coasts with a network of trading posts whose easternmost outpost by 1557 was Macau on the southern Chinese coast. With this, the gateway to Asia was open to Europeans for good.

The second important development in the sixteenth century was the previously mentioned empire-building that took place within the Islamic world, a development that was directly linked to earlier European expansion. Almost simultaneously, the European powers established empires overseas during the sixteenth century while vast continental empires in Asia either emerged or entered the mature phase of their development (such as the Ottoman empire or the Chinese Ming dynasty). The Ottoman expansion advanced aggressively against the Christian world at the very moment that the Spanish troops of the Habsburg emperor Charles V conquered the Aztec empire in Mexico. In a certain sense, the Ottoman empire pushed the European countries all around the Mediterranean to go overseas. Instead of referring to "European expansion," it makes far more sense to recognize the concurrence of expansion movements throughout all of Eurasia, which in most cases led to the establishment of larger political units. What these expansion movements had in common was the rapid deployment of the new artillery technology. Within a few decades firearms, their manufacturers, and gun crews were being exported from Europe across political and cultural borders to many remote corners of Asia.[12] German and Hungarian cannoneers helped the Turks conquer Constantinople in 1453, and artillery was becoming decisive in battles everywhere, such as in 1526 when the Moghul conqueror Baber defeated the army of the Sultan of Delhi. One of the major factors leading to the conquest of Mexico in 1519–21 was that the Spanish were armed with muskets and cannons. Granted, the revolution in military technology should not be interpreted as the only reason that such expansion drives took place simultaneously, but it was a generally applicable one, and it spread throughout the world from Europe. In other words, all of the empires of the sixteenth century were "gunpowder empires."[13]

Third, whereas in Asia the Europeans integrated themselves into the existing networks of trade and commerce and became participants in power struggles that had begun before their arrival, their expansion throughout the Western Hemisphere followed a thoroughly different pattern. The common catchall expression of "European expansion" easily camouflages these differences. The destruction of indigenous political structures, which began immediately after the discovery of America in 1492, or the expulsion of native peoples into the "wilderness," meant that the newcomers to America rarely had to make any compromises with them.[14] Politics in the New World were "white man's politics." European settlers brought with them their customs and institutions, languages and religions, and founded neo-European offshoot societies. The prerequisites for this approach were created in the sixteenth century; by the seventeenth century such societies had crossed the threshold to irreversible stability nearly everywhere.

Fourth, the Europeans introduced new life forms into America. Unknowingly, they brought germs of infectious disease against which the indigenous populations had no immunity. Among the many factors that facilitated the European conquest of the continents, none was as important as the disastrous smallpox epidemic that decimated the native population. Plants and animals also crossed the Atlantic in both directions; flora and fauna changed in Europe as well as in the Americas. Similar to what was later experienced in Australia during the eighteenth century, the New World now found itself connected to a Eurasian-African sphere, thousands of years old, in which certain biotypes flourished. At the same time, the Old World profited from the wealth of biological diversity in the Americas and the domestication talents of its original inhabitants. A clear-cut tally sheet of the costs and benefits involved cannot be drawn up. New crops—corn and potatoes in Europe—improved the life of many societies, whereas new pests tormented them. American plants soon reached Asia and Africa. Types of high-yield rice, peanuts, or cacao soon became extremely important for the economy. Several societies so thoroughly adapted to the new opportunities that their character completely changed in the process. Such was the case, for example, among the native inhabitants of the Great Plains west of the Mississippi River. The Spanish introduced them to horses, the French to firearms. Only after these people obtained horses were they able to hunt galloping buffalo. So began the characteristic horse-buffalo culture of the prairie Indian tribes.[15]

Fifth, another innovation appeared around 1500 that had global consequences—the printing press. In China, the technology of mechanically reproducing texts by way of woodblock printing had been known for centuries. It bestowed upon the literary culture of the upper classes, who were also in charge of administering the affairs of state, a particularly high degree of coherence. In European civilization, the invention of the printing press with moveable type made it possible to quickly and broadly publicize reports in Europe on the newly discovered and colonized areas overseas and, vice versa, to disseminate the rapidly growing pool of information accumulated by the European "scientific community" as far away as European ships could sail. This constituted an important advantage for Europeans, because Gutenberg's technology made it easier for them to develop potentially unlimited spheres of communication than it was for cultures dependent on handwritten forms of communication. If we keep in mind how this historical era started, the famous question of "how modern is the modern age?" can be answered very easily from the perspective of globalization. The discovery and colonization of America, the advance of European traders and soldiers in the Indian and Pacific oceans, the "ecological imperialism" and the "revolutions" in military and communication technology created the prerequisites for the expansion of existing spheres of interaction and the formation of new ones.

One of the new spheres of interaction was the Atlantic.[16] This was the only maritime sphere in which the Europeans met no seafaring competitors or adversaries, unlike in the eastern oceans, where there were Arabs, Chinese, Malays, and other maritime traders and pirates. From the beginning, the Atlantic was easy to navigate. Starting with Columbus, it became indisputedly a European lake in which Europeans alone warred with each other. There were no port cities to which each country first had to negotiate access. In the territories farther inland they met with little local resistance. Even the most complex statelike organizations, namely, the empires of the Aztecs and the Incas, fell within a fairly short time under the assaults of the Spanish. Nowhere did the Europeans come up against an opponent that was their equal, one that might have put a damper on their ambitions. From the European perspective, America was from the very beginning the continent of "unlimited possibility," a region easily available for colonial development. Only there was it possible to conduct one of the most ambitious experiments in social engineering of the early modern era: the establishment of slave plantations. Such plantations first appeared on a noticeable scale in the 1580s and came to full bloom in the 150-year period following 1680.[17] Where plantations flourished most— namely the Caribbean islands, Brazil, and the southeastern regions of North America—they became the dominant social institution. They produced sugar and tobacco for European markets, as the purchasing power of Europeans gradually increased, and they were dependent on the constant importation of enslaved Africans.[18] The slave trade took root in West Africa and became an important economic factor for several regions. The supply of slaves, who were then sold to British, Dutch, Portuguese, or French ship captains, was a secondary motive for a number of the wars that shaped the early modern history of the Atlantic coast of Africa. Starting around 1600, the "gunpowder revolution" also made its mark here.[19] Likewise, the manner in which some of the slave revolts took place in America is reminiscent of African methods of warfare.

The migration of Africans caused by the Atlantic slave trade represented a new level and intensity of integration, for it was the continual and regular transportation of a mass "commodity" (approximately 10.2 million Africans survived the Atlantic crossing between 1450 and 1870).[20] Unlike the traditional Eurasian trade by ship or caravan, this new form of trade did not link any existing centers of civilization but arose in close connection with the establishment of new forms of social and political organization. Among the various driving forces and interests, the greatest was the merchant capitalism of Western Europe—geographically a "third" force. The Atlantic slave trade created causal relations that linked Angolan villages with Brazilian sugar plantations, which in turn were linked to European tea salons. The trade rubbed shoulders with neighboring market systems, such as the "oriental" slave trade that was set up in the Islamic Middle East and the slave trade within the United States.

Other long-distance commercial links involved the exportation of spices, fine cloth, and tea from the eastern, southeastern, and southern regions of Asia to Europe by the big Dutch and English trading companies and the trade in furs that were supplied by native trappers in Canada and Siberia, traded among numerous middlemen, and eventually sold to customers in Europe and China. The first truly global trading network resulted from the silver mined in the Spanish colonies in America.[21] First it filled the Spanish treasuries, and from there it flowed into the coffers of those with whom Spain did business, both Europeans and Asians. Another route was through the journeys of the Manila galleons from Mexico and Peru to the Philippines, also colonized by the Spanish. From there, silk purchases were made in China. The influx of silver into the otherwise rather impermeable Chinese economy was so immense, particularly during the eighteenth century, that it encouraged long-lasting monetization, commercialization, and general rejuvenation within the Chinese empire.[22] The trade with precious metals created the first "flows" that circled the entire globe.

Holes in the Net

When studying this period ending roughly in the mid-eighteenth century, should we emphasize the moments of growing global integration that herald future developments or stress the holes in the network that speak for a lack of globality? This is a question that cannot be definitely answered on the basis of factual knowledge but only through careful evaluation of this knowledge. We choose here to point out the contradictoriness found in the tendencies of the period.

Undeniably, the trend toward greater integration was becoming stronger, not weaker, although this pertained only to expanding regions and not the entire world. Integration continued to take place within the well-established frameworks of large empires, religious ecumenes, and loosely woven networks of long-distance trade (in the modern form of "trading empires"). The world was coming together but only very slowly. Although cities flourished in several civilizations and a creative milieu of increasingly self-confident merchants evolved, as Fernand Braudel has vividly described,[23] the influence of long-distance trade was very small compared to that of locally and regionally produced and consumed goods. Only a very few places on earth could attribute their wealth to such long-distance trade, the leading one being the Netherlands. Except for the slave societies of America, economies were hard to find that produced goods almost exclusively for exportation. Economic crises did not spread from country to country and from continent to continent, and it was not a grave problem not to be economically integrated. Indeed, autarky was a very natural state for large, fairly developed regions, the most prominent being Japan and China. If similar trends in development existed in neighboring regions, they were caused less by diffusion—the most outstanding exception being the spread of firearms—and by chain reactions than by conditions that had a general impact overall, such as climatic changes (much like the "small Ice Age" believed to have occurred between about 1450 and 1850) or basic demographic trends. Such conditions had a greater influence than local factors and did not require the immediate contact between various communities.

The world was still polycentric. Although Western Europe did indeed initiate the fundamental transformation of the Atlantic, it remains uncertain whether the newly integrated and exploited colonial peripheries on American and Asian shores contributed substantially to the gradually growing prosperity in Europe.[24] Put rather bluntly, Britain did not become the land of the Industrial Revolution because it possessed sugar-producing islands in the Caribbean and collected taxes in Bengal. Europeans had not yet become the uncontested movers and shakers of the planet, economically speaking. At best, the European powers exported their political models to their own colonies. These proved to last only in those colonies where the settlers rebelled against European colonial governments in the name of established European principles, such as happened in the British parts of North America starting in the 1760s. Prior to 1800, only one ruler of significance attempted with great determination and on his own accord to reform his country according to his selective perception of Western European models: Peter the Great, of Russia. Otherwise, the shining example of the "West" found little reflection elsewhere. This was also true in reverse. At the point when European intellectuals were most enthusiastic and enthralled with China, that is, in the decades around 1700, several of them did indeed believe Europe could learn something from the Middle Kingdom about maintaining peace and the rational administration of government; yet nothing materialized from such suggestions. In the daily rhythm of the wealthy classes in Europe, exotica and colonial goods were becoming increasingly important. Naturally, they had a cultural impact.

When people became coffee drinkers or had a Chinese pavilion built in the palace garden, this reflected how they saw themselves in the world. But large sectors of the population were influenced by the consumption of foreign goods only after tea became a drink of the masses in England during the second half of the eighteenth century and the sugar used to sweeten it also enjoyed continually growing demand.[25]

During the early modern period, relations in matters of high culture were also developed to a lesser degree than they were in the nineteenth century. The European civilization was the only one to send travelers throughout the world and to accumulate an impressive knowledge about the languages, religions, customs, and political orders of other countries. This was an important cultural achievement and later gave Europe a great deal of knowledge used to rule its colonies.[26] Outside Europe, interest in foreign lands remained relatively small. Around 1750 a member of the Chinese court or even that of the Sultan in Istanbul knew much less about Europe than vice versa. Therefore, we can only speak of cultural interaction in a very limited sense. The cultural transfer from east to west remained insignificant simply because Asia sent so few visitors to Europe. In about 1700 the German philosopher Gottfried Wilhelm Leibniz, in cooperation with French friends, designed a plan for an academy of sciences in which European and Chinese scholars could cooperate. Objections on both sides prevented the realization of this thoroughly modern-sounding project. During the early modern period, Europe no longer received technological innovations of any significance from Asia. However, in several technically sophisticated crafts, Asia partially retained its earlier advantage over Europe well into the eighteenth century. A good example of this was high-quality porcelain, which was exported in large quantities from China to Europe.

Except in the Spanish colonies in America and the Philippines, Christian missionaries from both denominations were not really successful in converting the rest of the world to Christianity, despite the heroic, truly intercontinental effort made by the Jesuits to spread the faith in East Asia, Vietnam, India, and the Americas. In the Islamic world this mission did not stand a chance; in Japan it failed dramatically as early as the beginning of the seventeenth century; in China the conversion of the masses did not succeed, and the few members of the elite who embraced the faith had no lasting impact. Islam was more successful as a missionary religion. Starting in the fifteenth century, it spread to large areas of Southeast Asia, along the east coast of Africa, and in a belt of land just south of the Sahara. What facilitated this expansion was less empire-building "with fire and sword" than long-distance trade, for Islamization spread repeatedly from bases on the coast where the Arabs traded. Discussions between priests and scholars of the various religions, such as those that took place at the court of the Moghul emperor Akbar in the 1570s, were not replicated elsewhere.[27] No exchange occurred between the various ecumenes at a higher level. Intolerance and religious persecution were widespread, nowhere more so than in the Christian countries.

Scholarly exchange between the civilizations seems to have been greater during the Middle Ages, at the height of

Arab erudition, than in later centuries. In China, a superficial interest in European astronomy and cartography flourished temporarily, but no conclusions affecting existing theories were drawn from this scientific knowledge.[28] In their colonies, Europeans learned something about languages, geography, and botanical taxonomies from the native populations. The great assemblage of knowledge in Europe about the nature and cultures of Asia would not have come about without indigenous assistance. In turn, the Japanese developed a keen interest in European medicine and science, about which they learned in their secluded country through Dutch books.

When do we see the first tender shoots of a budding global consciousness? Today, globalization theorists consider such an awareness of globality to be an indication of the start of a new age. However, this view needs to be qualified. When a person in one of the most remote corners of the globe watches the television broadcast of a wedding of European royalty, this certainly reflects a more primitive form of global consciousness than when a person purchases a refrigerator containing a low level of pollutants in order to help protect the earth's ozone layer. This sense of global responsibilities assumes the existence of real causal effects of which people were not aware in the early modern period.

However, during this period people were able to envision the world more globally. Such a global picture developed among intellectuals in Europe. For a while, it could only be found in occidental civilization, which was the first to accept the concept of the earth as a sphere. The sailing expedition under the command of Fernão de Magalhães

(Magellan) from 1519 to 1522 was the first to circumnavigate the globe and thereby prove the validity of this concept. As a result of centuries of travel, colonization, and the tireless recording of everything discovered in the process, scholars and the educated classes of Europe were well informed about nearly all parts of the world as it existed around 1770, except for Australia, New Zealand, the African interior, and the western territories of North America. The charting of lands and seas advanced rapidly. After James Cook had completed three sailing expeditions around the world, the Anglo-Irish philosopher and parliamentarian Edmund Burke spoke of "a Great Map of Mankind" that lay spread out before Europe's educated classes.[29] At the same time, the history of the world began to be recorded based on empirical material available to all and no longer simply in the form of speculative, theological writings. This new historiography assumed that all of humankind shared a fundamental homogeneity and that all civilizations were approximately equal in value. Such attitudes flourished in Europe alone at the time. There, one was not yet as strongly convinced of the superiority of one's own civilization over all others, as one would be starting in the late eighteenth century. International law (a European invention of the seventeenth century) at first regulated only affairs among the European powers, but a philosopher such as Immanuel Kant, in his *Perpetual Peace: A Philosophical Essay* (1795), already recognized the necessity for a genuine order to guarantee world peace. Adam Smith and other economists in Scotland, England, and France began to perceive the world as a single interrelated economic sphere. The first translations of works from the Orient, particularly Antoine Galland's vastly popular translation of Arabian stories from *The Arabian Nights* (1704–17), introduced the European reading public to Eastern cultures. From the end of the eighteenth century onward, many works were translated from Persian, Chinese, or the rediscovered Sanskrit. The only other country in the eighteenth century to exhibit an interest in the outside world that was even remotely comparable to that of Europe was Japan, although it sent no travelers of its own out into the world. However, not until the mid-nineteenth century did translations of Western literature really become important there.[30]

1750–1880: Imperialism, Industrialization, and Free Trade

Early World Politics and Atlantic Revolutions

Historians often refer to the second half of the eighteenth century as an era in which a "double revolution" ushered in the "modern world." The first of these was the Industrial Revolution, starting in England about 1760; the second was the French Revolution of 1789, which introduced a new age of political order initially in Europe and later throughout the world. To be sure, the political revolution only gradually had an impact on the world, and the industrial revolution required more than a century to affect all of the areas that are productive industrial countries today. From the perspective of globalization, it is possible to analyze this development from a different starting point. We have seen that major integrative thrusts occurred over large areas in the eighth, thirteenth, and sixteenth centuries. By the middle of the eighteenth century, another such advance was under way. It began just before the "double revolution" and was fueled by the dynamics of state-building and preindustrial colonialism.

During the early modern period, the Europeans managed to take control of the world's seas, although no one

European power held a dominant position over its competitors. The Portuguese, Spanish, Dutch, English, and French, and even multinational pirate crews, were far superior to every other sea power. European naval supremacy extended to all branches of high-seas navigation: exploration, commerce, and warfare. Starting with the powerful Mediterranean republics of Venice and Genoa, the ties between naval power and commercial shipping were closer in Europe than they had ever been in any civilization in history. Spanish galleons loaded with silver crossed the Atlantic accompanied by war vessels. Both the Portuguese and the Dutch were able to gain a foothold in Asia and maintain it thanks to their naval artillery. The role of navies acquired a completely new dimension as instruments of the early modern state, and following the destruction of the Spanish Armada in 1588, naval warfare between the European powers became a means of conflict equal in importance to land warfare. Much of Europe's innovative talent was spent on perfecting naval and navigation techniques and in establishing and running such complex organizations as the Dutch Verenigde Oostindische Compagnie, the British East India Company, and the Royal Navy. Once Europe had secured control of the high seas, the stage was set for the rise of the most dynamic economic sector in the eighteenth century, the Caribbean-American plantation economy. Moreover, shipbuilding and shipping became important economic sectors each in its own right.

At first, the military branch of seafaring was subordinate in importance to commercial shipping. Around the middle of the eighteenth century, however, it emancipated itself from its supporting role and became the instrument of a form of politics unknown until then, namely, an early form of world politics.[1] On occasion, tensions between European countries had already exploded into minor military conflicts in the colonies. The new dimension of such conflict was that the strongest adversaries considered the entire world to be a theater of war. Accordingly, they shipped large infantry units overseas. Britain pioneered this new strategic concept, both in theory and in practice. During the Seven Years' War (1756–63), which was ignited and fought primarily in central Europe, British forces drove the French out of Canada (in the French and Indian War), fought them and their indigenous allies in India, and attacked Manila and Havana, two of the wealthiest cities in the Spanish colonial empire.[2] Then and later, the greater part of the British fleet remained stationed in domestic waters in order to protect the British Isles from enemy invasion, but even relatively minor victories overseas had far-reaching effects at home. The same phenomenon repeated itself in the larger conflict between Britain and revolutionary, later Napoleonic, France from 1793 to 1815. At the end of this second, truly global war, many strategically vital ports were in British hands, including Gibraltar, Malta, the Cape of Good Hope, and what would become Singapore. During this war the British completed their military conquest of India and attempted for the very first time to establish diplomatic relations with China. Shortly before, in 1788, Australia became the destination of the first British penal transports, thus turning the continent into yet another colony of the United Kingdom.

The improved capacity for naval warfare was one of the results of British efforts to rationally organize the state's policies of taxation and debt financing. As a "fiscal-military state," Britain was capable of mobilizing a greater amount of financial resources at home than were the "absolutistic" monarchies of the Eurasian continent. France and (with less determination) Russia quickly copied the British model, whereas the Asian empires of the era were falling behind Europe militarily even before the Industrial Revolution.

The concentration of power in the Atlantic region was one of the most important reasons for the great crisis of the Western Hemisphere.[3] In the 1760s both the British state and the Spanish crown, which had undergone a modernization process in the name of the Enlightenment, attempted to strengthen their respective holds over their American colonies. In response thirteen British colonies declared their independence in 1776 and fought against the British in a war that ended in the defeat of the former rulers in 1783. In the Spanish colonies the first attempts by the Creole elite to free themselves proved too weak, but they finally succeeded in becoming independent after the Spanish monarchy fell apart in the wake of Napoleon's invasion. By 1825 the Spanish colonial empire had disappeared altogether from the American continent. In the meantime a third war of independence had started in 1791 when the calls for liberty echoing from the French Revolution were picked up by the mulatto planters and black slaves in St. Dominique, then the most important sugar-producing area of the world. Following a civil war and French-British intervention, the land won its independence in 1804 under the name of Haiti, the first black republic in history.

The crises in the Atlantic that went back and forth between the Old and New Worlds from about 1765 to 1825 were the result of intense processes of integration in this maritime region. The long-term consequences were paradoxical. On the one hand, the revolts of settlers and slaves had a disintegrating and deglobalizing impact in that they destroyed some of the existing links. Once its sugar-exporting economy collapsed, slave-free Haiti dropped out of the global economy and has still not been reintegrated. In the United States the political elite directed the nation's attention westward, away from the Atlantic, and began the great adventure of settling the North American continent. The new republics of South and Central America wanted to have as little to do with Spain as possible. On the other hand, new international links were forged between the two sides of the Atlantic. In place of Spain, Latin American countries established new economic relations with the aspiring leader of globalization, Britain, and even the economic, social, and cultural relations between the United States and the British Isles survived the political split and developed over time into the "special relationship" that continues to exist today.

Although the United States refrained from becoming involved in international affairs any more than it absolutely had to during the entire nineteenth century, this did not prevent it from claiming very early—as if in ideological anticipation of its role in the twentieth and twenty-first centuries—to be a model for the rest of the world. The country did this with greater moral conviction than had revolutionary France, which quickly reverted to dictatorship and monarchy. Napoleon's short-lived empire reached the height of its power around 1810, uniting Europe for a brief historical moment, yet leaving no enduring vestiges except in places where it had directly or indirectly initiated legal and political reforms, such as in the states of the Confederation of the Rhine and in Prussia. If Napoleon Bonaparte's actions had any global repercussions, then it was by way of his invasion of Egypt in 1798. This invasion of what was then part of the Ottoman empire alarmed the entire Muslim world and also spurred British imperialism on to further expansion in Asia.[4]

The Far-reaching Impact of the Industrial Revolution

What changes occurred in long-distance economic relations as a result of the spread of industrialization? There are many definitions of the Industrial Revolution, no fewer attempts to explain it, and a lively debate over the question of whether the socioeconomic and ecological changes associated with this term were abrupt and fundamental enough to justify labeling it a "revolution" to begin with.[5] The Industrial Revolution did not cause a sudden change in intercontinental economic relations. The revolution originated in one quite small economic sphere and spread gradually and unevenly around the world. Particularly interesting from the standpoint of the history of globalization are the following five aspects.

First, the Industrial Revolution began in Britain, a country that already enjoyed an unusually well-developed network of foreign trade relations and colonial connections. Still, this in itself was not a necessary and defining prerequisite of the Industrial Revolution; otherwise the revolution would have started in the Netherlands. Throughout history, major impulses have often arisen in the peripheral regions of the civilized world, as was mentioned in the previous chapter with regard to the rise of Islam. The Industrial Revolution, however, occurred in what was already a well-developed center of dynamic economic development. Granted, evidence has also been found outside of northwestern Europe, particularly in southern and eastern Asia, for a so-called "industrious revolution"— meaning a mobilization of previously unused labor for marketable but not yet industrial production, a mobilization spurred on by an increasingly individualized consumer demand. This industrious revolution appears to have reached the limits of its potential in the eighteenth century, due in good part to the evident impact of political crises and the lack of an efficiently operating financial system and particularly of legal institutions to protect private ownership and property.[6]

Second, the Industrial Revolution did not emerge from within a self-contained economic system, as is evident in its leading economic sector, the cotton industry of northern England. This industry was a side effect of existing global contacts insofar as it strove to compete with the quantitatively and qualitatively superior Indian textiles produced for the British market. From the very beginning, the cotton industry was involved in global markets. All of its raw material, cotton, had to be imported from abroad, and as early as the 1830s textiles comprised more than

70 percent of Britain's exports.[7] British business also had global contacts in the Atlantic slave economy. The impact of such involvement on the Industrial Revolution, though probably not decisive, was considerably greater than has been previously thought.[8]

Third, since there was only one Industrial Revolution, what followed in its wake were numerous industrialization processes within national, regional, or international frameworks. Such processes of industrialization continue to take place today, especially in Asia. In certain societies this has gone on until their economies entered a postindustrial stage of development; others without industry were able to achieve wealth by specializing in the export of agricultural products (Denmark, New Zealand) or in oil production. A third, very large group of countries cannot be expected to develop a globally competitive industrial sector in the foreseeable future. Thus, it cannot be said that industrialization is an "all-inclusive" global process analogous to the spread of television or Western consumer tastes. However, it was and is a motor for integration in other areas.

Fourth, industrial means of production did not spread simply by imitation of the British model. We must imagine it more as a "complex process of creative adaptation."[9] Even the second generation of industrializing countries—Belgium, Switzerland, France, Germany, and the United States—lacked some of the important conditions inherent in British development, such as a foregoing "agricultural revolution" in which the class of small independent farmers was wiped out. Therefore, these other countries were forced to seek new solutions. Thoroughly independent of

Western influence, Japan developed institutions advantageous to its industrialization as early as the seventeenth and eighteenth centuries, although it did not actually begin to industrialize until around 1880 and is therefore considered to be part of the third generation, along with Russia.

Fifth, it took quite a while for the industrial means of production to prevail in the economy and for its attendant phenomena to become predominant in society. Not until roughly 1820 did Britain become the first country in which nearly all areas of life were influenced by industry—except politics, where the agrarian nobility and aristocratic financiers remained more influential than bourgeois manufacturers and industrialists. Nearly everywhere in Europe, small areas of regional industry arose like islands of dynamic development within agricultural environments. Except for Japan, the situation in Asia looked quite different. By 1900 nothing close to a coherent industrial system existed, only a scattering of factories here and there. The same was true in Africa, whose sole economic significance for the global economy stemmed from gold and diamond mining in South Africa.

Important for globalization was not merely the fact that factories were using steam engines and mechanization to produce an increasing supply of consumer goods, such as cotton textiles, at decreasing cost. Equally significant was the mass production of complicated, mechanized equipment and machinery. The most important of these were steamships, trains, and more accurate and destructive guns and cannons. In the mid-nineteenth century, the impact of the industrialization of war and transportation was felt far from the centers of industrial production. Whereas industries were only established in areas where a number of natural, technological, political, and social resources and conditions converged, many of their products spread from Europe and North America throughout the entire world. This was possible because, firstly, effective trading networks already existed in and between many economies that could be more intensively used to expand global trade further. Secondly, the use of steamships drastically reduced the transportation costs of long-distance trade for mass goods and products of heavy industry over the long run. Thirdly, in many urban centers of the world, a demand gradually emerged for those prestige-conferring goods that were emblematic of Western civilization.

Firearms produced in Europe had reached the interior of both Africa and North America before the Industrial Revolution. The industrialization of arms production had contradictory effects. On the one hand, it increased the output and made weapons, particularly light ones, more readily available. On the other, the best products of the arms industry, such as heavy artillery and the slowly emerging warships built from iron, were becoming more and more expensive. The previously "democratic" world of muskets now split into two, namely, the world consisting of those governments (the "great powers") who could afford the most modern weapons produced by Krupp or Vickers and those who could not. The correlation between technology and power was evident on other, less consequential levels. A gun simply built could be repaired by an African or Indian village blacksmith. However, the Maxim gun, invented in 1884 and immediately deployed in colonial wars, almost never reached the hands of the "natives" and gave the imperialist user an incomparable advantage. (This advantage was not eliminated until the submachine gun was invented at the end of World War I and spread throughout the world, thus causing a renewed democratization of violence.)

Even more important was the industrialization of transportation, specifically the use of steam energy to mechanize movement.[10] The 1830s brought a breakthrough for the steamship, which had first proved its utility in inland and coastal waters. Transatlantic steamship travel began to occur on a regular basis. Steamships even appeared in non-Western countries, such as in 1835 on the Euphrates, and as early as 1850 a steamship was traveling for the first time from Shanghai to London. The age of the sailing ship ended in the twenty-year period between 1860 and 1880. The opening of the Suez Canal in 1869, built primarily for steamship use, halved the time it took to travel from London to Bombay and may be considered the symbolic demarcation of the era. The major freight routes were in place by the end of this period. Whereas in the eighteenth century sugar had been the most important commodity traded in overseas commerce, now huge amounts of wheat, rice, cotton, and coal were being shipped across the seas. For decades most of the vessels hauling this produce were built in English shipyards.

Originally, railway transportation served only local and regional purposes. It is not particularly important to note the dates when the first functioning locomotive began to operate in every country but rather when the railways started to shape each society. In this sense, the age of the railroad began in Europe in the mid-1840s. By the turn of the century, railway transportation had made an impact on only a few non-European countries, most of all India, Argentina, and Japan. China, South Africa, and Turkey were in the middle of major, internationally financed projects of railway construction. Even if the rails were laid as much for military as for economic purposes, as in India, the effect was still the same: wherever a railway was built, it helped integrate the region into international commerce. Major technical challenges, such as the Transcontinental Railroad connecting the eastern and western coasts of the United States in 1867, extended the influence of urban centers to areas previously inaccessible. When Jules Verne published his novel *Around the World in Eighty Days* in 1873, the book's popularity could be attributed to this incredible innovation that enabled a person to cross gigantic continental expanses quickly. Only eccentrics undertook such adventures, but the tourist had already begun to replace the traveler. Organized group excursions to the Ottoman empire and North Africa were nothing special or exotic any longer. Even in Japan, which had been almost hermetically sealed off from the outside world until 1853, the first hotel for foreigners opened in 1860, complete with a wine cellar and a billiard table.

The technological invention to have the most dramatic effects on globalization during this era was the telegraph.[11] After all, cables are easier to lay than railroad tracks. The history of telegraphy began in 1839 with Samuel Morse's first patent. By 1866 the first truly functioning transatlantic cable was in use, and by about 1880 a telegram could be sent from London to any relatively significant place in the entire British empire, whatever the continent. Thanks to the telegraph, the speed with which news was transmitted between Europe and the United States increased by a factor of ten thousand. At the same time, the speed of sending information was decoupled from that of shipping goods, which extremely accelerated developments on the financial and commodities markets. Even diplomats and colonial agents were now to report more often for instructions from their respective ministries.[12] At the same time, the volume of mail service increased tremendously thanks to the transportation of mail by rail, a drastic reduction of postage fees in several countries, the first steps in establishing a modern postal service in other countries, and the easing of communication across national borders through international agreements.[13]

Empires and Nation-States

The two major political "grand designs" to evolve out of the mid-century, liberalism, with its free trade philosophy, and Marxism, were utopias of globalization in which the nation-state was given no more than a subordinate role as a political force. Radical free traders like Richard Cobden hoped to create a prosperous and peaceful world for all humankind once trade restrictions had been eliminated everywhere, a world enveloped in interaction yet free from conflict. Free traders believed such a world would be possible once states and governments stopped intervening in the voluntary agreements between individuals.[14] Karl Marx also considered the state and politics to be secondary and superficial phenomena. In his opinion, history was shaped by the force of increasingly global capitalism and its internal contradictions on the one hand, and that of the proletarians of the world uniting in revolution, on the other.

Part of the design of free traders was indeed implemented when Britain unilaterally repealed its most important duties in 1846. Other states soon followed suit, and by 1870 all of Europe west of the Czarist empire had become a free trade zone. Outside of Europe, however, the establishment of the antipolitical utopia of global free trade required political and military intervention. Britain, by far the world's leading colonial power, introduced free trade to its colonies. From then until the mid-1930s, it did not establish any insurmountable obstacles to block the business of third parties in its empire.[15] Despite the British example, large, non-European empires and states were not readily willing to abandon their own traditional orders and join in the effort of establishing a world of "free" trade. In the cases of the Ottoman empire, China, Japan, and Siam (Thailand), such initial protest was overcome through pressure or military force (e.g., the Opium War against China, 1839–42). "Unequal treaties" opened up markets that previously had been closed to products of European industry. Behind such free trade imperialism was a program that went beyond the integration of these regions into the global economy.[16] Traditional monarchies in Asia were also expected to conduct themselves in a "civilized" international manner and to become useful if not at first equal members of the "family of nations." Except in Muslim societies, this also implied the right of Christian missionaries to pursue their calling. Where possible, these "barbarian" countries, as they were sometimes called, were to adapt their domestic institutions to resemble the Western model.

In those places where Europe and the United States attempted directly to export their institutions as part of such a "civilizing mission," they met with little success in this period. This was true in the colonies as well as in subordinate but independent countries. The basic fact that liberal, if not democratic, colonial powers like Britain and France set up truly authoritarian systems in their colonies prevented permanent transfer of institutions. Such a transplantation of institutions only succeeded in places where the indigenous elite systematically adopted elements of the European social model. Without exception, such self-reform was also the path toward political independence. In the "white dominions" of the British empire (Canada, Australia, New Zealand), no one ever considered seceding from the motherland in a way resembling the New England rebellion of 1776. However, no one was willing to submit to the dictates of the motherland, either. By the end of the nineteenth century, the dominions of Canada and Australia were sufficiently independent to introduce protective tariffs within the empire. At the same time, these societies developed their own political systems to such an extent that they were more democratic, more egalitarian, and simply more "modern" than Britain's own system. Thus, the dominions are among the "success stories" of the nineteenth century, economically and politically speaking. As in all settler societies (including the United States), the indigenous peoples were not allowed to enjoy the fruits of such success and were considerably worse off than in colonies without a large European settler community.

The second pioneer of modernization outside of Europe was Japan. Opened to the world only in 1853–54 as the result of a U.S. naval action, the country started down the path of resolute self-reform following the 'Meiji Restoration' of 1868. During this period of reform, Western elements were adopted on a grand scale and then mixed with authentic or cleverly invented domestic traditions. Japan did not become a genuine democracy (even in Europe, these were still hard to find), but in the 1880s it did become the first constitutional state in Asia. Core institutions of social life such as the family remained Japanese, while more formal institutions such as the military, police, governmental administration, and universities either were restructured along the lines of carefully selected Western models or, in some cases, introduced for the first time. Seldom was the foreign model left in its original form. By the turn of the century, Japan was already being called, depending on the preference of the observer, the "Britain of the East" or the "Prussia of Asia."

An entire civilization can undergo such collective self-transformation only if it is subjected to immense external pressure to adapt, while retaining a certain measure of self-determination. During the nineteenth century the pressure to adapt was felt throughout the world, and it is here that we come closer to discovering the motor that powered the globalization processes in this era. Once a single country, namely, the United Kingdom, had established itself economically as the world's most dynamic force featuring the highest standard of living per capita and attractive, free institutions, every other society, in comparison, was a latecomer and potential imitator. In a sense, this hierarchy was inevitable because Britain possessed a worldwide dominion of the seas, an extensive intervention force, and the world's most lucrative colonies. Moreover, its political and educated classes were convinced that theirs was the most advanced and most exemplary civilization on earth. Corroborated in equal measure by its religion and its scientific achievements, Britain saw itself as both model and ordained policing power of the world. Meanwhile, France continued to fascinate the world (particularly eastern Europe and the southern Mediterranean) with its cultural glamour and a capital city that became the quintessence of sophisticated living. This only helped increase the attraction of Western Europe for the rest of the world. With its image tarnished by slavery and civil war until 1865, the United States was preoccupied with itself and kept its distance from the rest of the world for most of the century; it would not achieve the stardom enjoyed by Britain until the twentieth century.

By the 1860s at the latest, no ruling group could afford to close its eyes to Britain's power, success, and determination to civilize the rest of the world. This led to a wave of reform movements everywhere from Latin America to the Ottoman empire, from Egypt to Siam, and even to the surprisingly cosmopolitan Madagascar. By taking at least some steps toward accommodating the British, ruling elites hoped to ensure a place for themselves and their countries in a world dominated by Western Europe, specifically Britain.[17] This globalization via adaptation, which Europe did not directly impose upon the world, was marked by a similar ambivalence between compliance and resistance, admiration and abhorrence, as is evident today in the relationship of the rest of the world to the United States. For the first time in history, a trend evolved toward unipolarity in the cultural realm—although less in that of power politics than is currently the case, because Britain was relatively weaker militarily around 1870 than the United States is at the start of the twenty-first century. Of all the known and conceivable paths of development, the Western European–British one seemed to promise the greatest success. Even in Europe, the tension between compliance and resistance became one of the most important catalysts of the building of nation-states. It appeared that only a homogeneous, rationally organized, and powerful nation-state could handle the new forces of the age. It is fairly irrelevant that most of the attempts to adapt the British model broke down or never even truly got started. What is relevant for the history of globalization is the new perspective from which the world viewed the British-dominated West. This view was, for the first time, underpinned by a universal history of progress of which every country could be a part and to which there no longer appeared to be any real alternative.

Still, the degree of cultural universalization that was actually achieved must not be exaggerated. It is very difficult to draw any definite conclusions here. Nationalism and nation-state–building made the Enlightenment's idea of the world citizen appear antiquated in Europe. More than ever before, science was housed within the university system of each nation. Only a few ever talked about "world literature" after Goethe's death in 1832, and "world history" was superseded by national histories. "World Expositions" were held on a fairly regular basis starting in 1851 but only in Europe or the United States. These expositions celebrated the technical and material feats and achievements of the "developed" peoples and those that "primitive" peoples (as they were called) had managed to accomplish with the help of the West. Also in 1851 Julius Reuter founded in London the world's first news agency. Within a decade he had set up a network of correspondents on six continents.[18] As the world became cabled, it became possible to supply the growing readership of daily newspapers with current news reports from around the world. About 1870 a modern press began to emerge in countries such as Japan, China, and Egypt, marking the beginning of a global trend in media development. Now, for the first time, people were witness to international media events. The Crimean War and the American Civil War were the first wars to be documented by special correspondents and photographers. At the same time, the Taiping Revolution in China received no attention from the newly evolved world public. Although this conflict was certainly no less dramatic than the others, almost no photographs of it exist. Other manifestations of Western high culture also spread to a similar degree worldwide, even if the performances of bel canto operas in Manaus, Istanbul, or Shanghai could not compete with the industrial production of cheap recordings in the twentieth century.

Even during this age of worldwide European dominance, Christianity failed to become the dominant religion.[19] The extraordinary dedication and effort of thousands of missionaries from both the Protestant and Catholic faiths and many different religious sects and orders (more than a few of which had begun their missions before the colonial conquest of these lands) bore no fruit in Asia. Christians remained a minority and gained no political influence anywhere, while Muslim missionaries successfully continued to convert people to Islam. Moreover, the map of the world's languages changed little. Following the colonial period, people continued to speak Spanish and Portuguese in South America, although Portuguese lost its role as *lingua franca* to English in maritime Asia around 1830. It should not be surprising that English rose to become the number one global language.[20] This resulted from the demographic expansion of the Anglophone United States, the success of the British Dominions, and the early expansion of the British into multilingual regions, such as India and South Africa, that were in need of a common language. In the twentieth century the triumphant advance of the English language (in its British and American variations) was also aided by the culture industry and the mass media.

The Emergence of a World Economy

During the age of free trade (1846–80), a significant number of economic relationships were established worldwide, usually unimpaired by governmental regulation. This development was the result of technological and political factors, as well as an understanding of governance in which the nation-state made a more absolute but also a much more circumscribed claim to intervene in society than in today's age of interdependent interventionist states. This did not result in a "global economy" as theorists define it today, that is, "an economy with the capacity to work as a unit in real time on a planetary scale."[21] Not even the advent of the telegraph, which has justifiably been called the "internet of the Victorian Age,"[22] could do this. However, economic growth ("capital accumulation") had been taking place within intercontinental structures since the sixteenth century, particularly those of plantation systems and Asian trade. So what was really new in the nineteenth century?

First, no one experienced globalization more intensively than those who settled in a foreign part of the world. In the course of the nineteenth century, "a new topography of cross-border migration"[23] evolved within Europe, which traditionally had had an unusually mobile population. People left southern, southeastern, and eastern Europe to move most often to Germany, France, and Switzerland. However, the significance of these migratory movements pales in comparison to the migrations that occurred in other parts of the world. It has been estimated that between 1850 and 1914, about 60–70 million people left their homelands, never to return. Among these were 40–45 million Europeans who emigrated overseas, primarily to North and South America, 7 million immigrants to Asian Russia, and 11 million Indians, Chinese, and Japanese, most of whom became contract laborers ("coolies") in foreign countries (Southeast Asia, the United States, the Caribbean, East and South Africa).[24] Although the slave trade shrank steadily once it was outlawed by the British parliament in 1807, no fewer than 2.7 million Africans were still sold as slaves to America between 1811 and 1867.[25] Immigrants seldom blended immediately into their new environment. They created ethnic communities—in extreme cases, self-sufficient "Chinatowns"—and thereby enhanced the multiethnic character of their adopted countries. Since the immigrants usually maintained contact with their homelands, the long-distance migration of the nineteenth century covered the globe with a netting of transoceanic kinship connections. The migrants also contributed economically to global integration. They settled the frontiers, were good customers for products from their homeland, increased the total global productivity by an efficient use of resources (division of labor, better locations), and often established new companies and branches of business. The rise and continual success of the United States as the world's leading economic power cannot be explained without acknowledging the contributions of immigrants during the nineteenth century.

Second, between 1800 and 1913 the volume of world trade increased twenty-five-fold. One major boom in the expansion of commerce started in the 1850s, followed by another extraordinary acceleration of growth starting in the mid-1870s. Indeed, world trade was growing much faster than world production.[26] However, three-fourths of all international trade was concentrated within Europe and within the triangle of Western Europe, North America, and Australia–New Zealand. The only colonies to become important economic subcenters were India and South Africa. The industrializing countries, led by Britain, were the masters and organizers of this new phase of worldwide economic integration. Still, niches of regional networks continued to flourish among Indian, Chinese, and Armenian merchants, just to name a few.[27] The global economy retained the rudiments of its earlier polycentrism.

Third, it was possible for the first time in history to transport mass commodities goods over long distances. One important turning point came around 1880. In 1875 the attempt to bring refrigerated American meat to Britain succeeded; by 1880 the amount of meat shipped reached 120,000 tons per year. At the end of the 1860s the United States was exporting 28 million (imperial) bushels of wheat, mostly to Europe; in the early 1880s it was 140 million bushels. Steamships, railways, refrigeration technology, and transatlantic telegraphy had now become mature technologies that could be employed profitably in the transcontinental distribution of bulky, low-value goods. Henceforth, the centers of production, trade, and consumption of commodities like wheat and meat were closely connected. Information on prices, supply, and demand now traveled considerably faster than did the goods themselves, a development that completely transformed long-distance trade and created a single world market.[28] The advancing integration of the Atlantic region began to make itself evident in an increasing convergence of commodity prices and real wages between Western Europe and North America. The decline of British grain production and the country's transition to exporting finished products and importing grain after the repeal of the Corn Laws in 1846 are the first examples of structural change caused by this new form of a global division of labor. Regional markets reacted to one another with hitherto unknown speed and sensitivity.[29]

Fourth, the most unmistakable indication of closer global

connections was the appearance of economic cycles that affected the entire world. The so-called Great Depression that began in 1873 caused the prices of goods to fall worldwide. Even more enduring was the favorable impact of an expansion in demand after 1896 on all continents: the first worldwide economic boom. While there continues to be much debate about the underlying causes of these fluctuations, it is clear that their effects now spread quickly and widely on increasingly integrated markets held together by efficient transport and communication networks. By the late nineteenth century, almost every place on earth was affected by global economic cycles.[30]

1880–1945: Global Capitalism and Global Crises

The Experience of Globality, Global Economy, and World Politics at the Turn of the Century

It has become commonplace in economic history to describe the decades preceding the outbreak of World War I as an era of extensive globalization, followed by a phase of deglobalization that ended only after World War II. If we investigate more than just economic integration, however, the contrast between the two phases becomes far less sharp. Instead, it becomes increasingly clear that, from this point on, conflict and cooperation, integration and disengagement were taking place on a global scale. There was simply no escaping one another; the world had become one large community with a shared destiny, as could be experienced in daily life. Since then, even processes of disintegration can only be described as developments within a global economy or system of world politics, because these processes had such far-reaching effects and were often conscious reactions to globalization.

The advent of the Internet was not the first development to make our world more accessible to more people.

Even earlier, in the decades prior to World War I, the planet was becoming the frame of reference for the thoughts, actions, and experiences of a rapidly growing percentage of the world's population. To a great extent, this was the result of an increasing ability to communicate across long distances. The United States, the birthplace of mass media, had always topped the statistics for literacy. After about 1870 the percentage of both illiterate men and women fell all over Europe, even in more backward regions such as Spain, Russia, and the Balkans. On the eve of war, governments had made sure that recruits everywhere could read their instructions and write their families from the front.[1] The literacy rate in Japan lagged only a little behind that of France or Germany. In the colonized parts of the world (with the exception of the British Dominions and several Latin American countries), the majority of the people remained illiterate, although everywhere modern, educated classes emerged who were able to read news reports from around the world in the English, French, or Spanish press. In China, Japan, Egypt, and Ottoman Turkey, the press flourished in the traditional languages, which were often simplified in the course of linguistic reform. Everywhere, journalism became established as a profession and journalists as a social group.[2]

Since the turn of the century, the world had been experiencing a fundamental transformation of the dimensions in which people lived and thought, particularly the way they experienced time and space, a transformation of which not only the elite were aware.[3] In 1884 twenty-five states agreed to divide the world into a system of time zones and establish global time based on the Greenwich meridian. By 1913 this system had been adopted almost everywhere.[4] Long beforehand, the Western world had undergone a chronometric transformation, and the inexpensive pocket watch had become a common commodity. The regiment of standardization introduced by mechanized timekeeping spread unceasingly.[5] Concurrently, the data provided by a network of weather stations installed worldwide made it possible for the first time to observe how local and regional weather systems were systematically linked within a "global climate." The "timber famine" that evolved at the turn of the century is an early example of the growing concerns about the finiteness of natural resources, which led to the first criticism of a global *Raubwirtschaft*, meaning an "exploitative and destructive economy."[6]

Confidence in the ability to overcome the obstacle of distance became commonplace. Such confidence was inspired on a grand scale by transcontinental steamship travel, which was just as indispensable for the elite of the global economy (although with far less assurance following the sinking of the *Titanic* in 1912) as for the underclasses of Chinese contract laborers. On a smaller scale, mobility increased with the help of new inventions such as the bicycle (not widespread in Europe until the 1880s), streetcar, bus, and automobile. In 1903 the world was amazed to witness the first motorized flight. In 1913 an airplane with eight people on board flew for two hours. It was then that the age of European geographic exploration ended. Once Roald Amundsen reached the South Pole in 1911, every part of the world had been explored and charted. Only the highest peaks on earth had so far resisted all advances by European Alpinists.

Such mastery of space and distance influenced the mind-sets and attitudes of the age. The present was increasingly perceived as the accumulation of simultaneously occurring events worldwide—that is, as global simultaneity instead of the immediate first-hand experience of people's own lives. In politics and business, science and art, there was a strong consensus that the mastery of distance and global simultaneity would bring about fundamental changes in how people lived together. With increasing frequency, globality was interpreted as being the starting point for transnational cooperation and solidarity. However, the easier it appeared to overcome distance, the broader was the horizon that needed to be scanned for possible enemies and competitors.

For many people, globalization first touched their daily lives through the effects of global economic integration. Since the 1880s at the latest, one spoke of one global economy as an interconnected entity.[7] In the years leading up to World War I, there was another thrust in worldwide economic integration, the results of which can be viewed in two ways. Either one describes the turn-of-the-century global economy as a multilateral system that cannot be broken down into smaller units, or one emphasizes the very different forms and effects that global economic integration had, depending on social situation and geographic location. If the former is assumed, then the global economy must be conceived as a complex entity that has little in common with the popular idea of the division of labor between the agrarian periphery and the Western industrial metropole. It is important to remember three points.

Firstly, the intercontinental flows of labor, capital, and goods were linked with and mutually influenced one another. The export of European capital financed the expansion of the global economic infrastructure. For decades private British citizens annually invested 5–7 percent of the British national product in foreign government securities, railway stock, and so on. This exported capital not only returned to Europe in the form of a worldwide demand for locomotives, sewer pipes, and generators, it worked continually to integrate new regions into the global economy where Europeans then settled and usually produced agricultural goods for export. Meanwhile, the interest income earned by those investing abroad covered the trade deficits incurred by European countries and enhanced the demand for imported goods. Industrial companies reacted to the geographic expansion of their markets by investing in plants with a capacity large enough to handle a volume of sales on a global scale, or they established plants abroad and transformed themselves into multinational corporations.[8]

Secondly, between 1870 and 1914 the loosely interconnected trading networks that were usually centered in London consolidated into a unified system. The most important indication of this development is that the balances of trade and payments were now settled multilaterally.[9] To imagine the world as being divided into "halves," in which globalization was limited to the Northern Hemisphere, is to ignore facts such as the impact of economic integration on non-European peoples and the dependence of seemingly bilateral trade on the multilateral settlement of payments.

Thirdly, the global economy could only function as a coherent system with the help of a well-developed infrastructure, which depended on initiatives taken by the nation-states. Transportation and communication infrastructures were financed privately to a far greater degree than one can imagine today. However, international rail transport, post, and telegraphy required that governments agree on technical standards and common procedures for such things as the unhindered transmission of telegraph signals across borders.[10] The international monetary system demonstrates the extent to which globalization was based on conditions created by national governments before 1914. Since the 1870s all important currencies had been based on the gold standard, so that global trade and investment could be conducted without being exposed very much to the risks of inflation and fluctuating exchange rates. Fundamental economic policy decisions were practically dictated by the gold standard, including the stipulation of currency stability, low government spending, and a free flow of capital. The reasons for the stability of this "international" monetary system, which was confined to Europe and the Atlantic, are still not quite clear. Certainly, the system itself was not "automatically" self-stabilizing. Like other institutions of this early stage of globalization, the gold standard was created and influenced by nation-states.[11]

Just as important as the multilateral, systemic nature of the global economy are the variety of types of integration into the world economy and the continued existence of gaping "holes in the net." Such holes included regions that had only sporadic contact with the global economy, like most of the African continent, the landlocked provinces of China, and regions on every continent that could not be reached by train or steamship. In other places, the effects of the global economic division of labor—meaning the simultaneous existence of technological-institutional homogenization and economic differentiation—were evident to varying degrees. In the European colonies as well as in the politically independent countries of Latin America, enclaves arose that were not at all integrated into the local economy but were instead geared completely to the world market. One such example were the tin mines in Malaya, where Chinese contract laborers, under the supervision of European engineers, extracted tin ore for export to the industrialized world before they returned to China with their hard-earned savings.[12] Global economic integration did not lead to any lasting structural change in this case. The same holds true for the plantations found everywhere throughout tropical Asia and Africa (coffee, tea, cacao, rubber, etc.) and for the guano collected off the Peruvian coast and exported as fertilizer. In several cases, particularly in Argentina, almost the entire economy was geared toward the exportation of agricultural products. In these export economies, which were highly susceptible to fluctuations in demand and prices on the world market, access to the global economy was not only a source of economic profit but also social status and political power.[13]

The industrial West was an area of extraordinarily intense economic interaction in which regional, national, international, and global networks overlapped. Global economic integration was not limited merely to business transactions beyond national borders; even what appeared to be strictly domestic developments, such as the opening up of the American West through the construction of railroads or the adoption of the gold standard by the German empire, had an immense impact on the global economy. The manufacture of consumer and producer goods exported worldwide was concentrated in the North Atlantic region, which was also the source of export capital, new forms of globally implemented company structure, and the most important technologies. Only in this region did larger sectors of society earn enough to allow them to consume more than just the necessities of life. In 1913 the estimated average annual income per capita in the United States and the British Dominions was $5,300 (basis: 1990), in Western Europe $3,500, in Japan $1,400, in the rest of Asia only $640, and in Africa (where the overall statistical representation was "enhanced" by South African mining) $585.[14] Even then, the disparity between the richest centers of the world—no longer to be found in Europe—and the poorest had already reached a ratio of 10:1. Around 1820 this ratio appears to have been 3:1.

It would be wrong to assume that globalization in the nineteenth century established links between coherent, integrated national economies and forced them to adapt. Instead, globalization occurred parallel and simultaneously to state-building. How did the two processes influence each other? Particularly important are the political reactions to the consequences of global economic integration. These came first from the "globalization losers," such as the German farmers who felt threatened by cheap imports of grain and meat from abroad. American farmers demanded that the United States abandon the gold standard, which depressed prices and thus increased their debt burdens. Likewise, the first wave of Canadian immigrants turned against the inflow of any more unskilled labor. Each of these groups demanded help from their respective governments to protect their interests. With the exception of Britain, most of the countries reverted to protectionism after 1878 (the United States had never abandoned it), and the first restrictions on immigration were established. In a period of increasing racism, these restrictions were first directed at Asian migrants.[15] In other words, just about the time that the global economy began to evolve, so too did the modern interventionist state. In fact, the latter developed to a degree in reaction to the former. This new type of state used tariff policy and, somewhat later, social policy in an attempt to steer globalization in a direction beneficial to "national" interests. Its political program did not originate with Cobden or Marx but with the Swabian-American journalist Friedrich List (1789–1846), a globally influential critic of globalization *avant la lettre*.

The new tariff walls were not high enough to endanger the recently created global economy.[16] Rather, the return to protectionism was both an indication and the cause of a change in the political climate. The permeation of politics by economic issues was evident everywhere and stood in sharp contrast to the mood that had been prevalent at mid-century. First and foremost, this was the politicization of globality. No longer were the consequences of globality being accepted unquestioningly as fate; instead they evolved into a topic for organized interest groups, who attempted to exert some influence on the political decisions being made in the parliaments of Western countries. The final decades of the "long" nineteenth century (ca. 1789–1914) were not only a period of globalization but also one of "territorialization," meaning the effort to tie social relations to specifically demarcated political-territorial spaces, usually to nation-states.[17] Global economic integration was now a means to enhance the power of the state, which would attain political legitimacy by favoring domestic interests. In this way, the issue of exercising political control over worldwide integration went from being a topic promoted by globalization losers to an offensively pursued aim of national and power politics.

Imperialism and World War

As communication and transportation networks spread and worldwide chains of production emerged, interaction and competition between territorial states began to take place on a global scale. It is one of the characteristics of the era that reflection on current affairs was predominantly cast in terms of global rivalries between armed forces, nation-states, national economies, or even entire civilizations. About 1900, for example, it seemed paradoxical to German proponents of *Weltpolitik* to consider the German empire as a "satiated" great power in the Bismarckian sense with no expansionist aims. The future, it was argued, belonged to world powers that controlled the population, raw materials, and markets of far-flung empires and were capable of projecting their power worldwide. Therefore, countries only had the choice between "decline or world power," and mere self-preservation required them to conduct power politics on a global scale.

The ability to overcome distance also opened the doors to the idea of the shortage of space. The average annual rate of population growth on earth had doubled during the years 1870–1913, compared with the period of 1820–70.[18] In 1913 the global population totaled 1.8 billion people, which does not seem very threatening now in light of the 6.3 billion inhabiting the earth today. However, this figure gave many at that time the opportunity to warn others of the shortage of "living space" and to predict fierce "struggles for land." The colossal movements of internal colonization in North America, Russian Siberia, and (beginning in 1890) Manchuria appeared to confirm such a finding. In the United States the trek westward to settle the territories there reached its final peak in the first decade of the twentieth century.[19] After that, the frontier was "closed." At the same time, the situation of the displaced Native Americans reached its bleakest point. Despite all the gloomy predictions, a great deal of unsettled land remained everywhere. With respect to demographic developments, the mood was worse than the actual situation.

In this atmosphere of imperialistic last-minute panic, growing international competition triggered a race to divide up the remaining parts of the world that had not yet been colonized. In 1880 a total of 25 million square kilometers were under the control of one of the major colonial powers (the Eurasian land-based empires not included); in 1913 this figure was 53 million.[20] Each expansionary move had its specific reason. Seldom did the visible economic potential of a region play a role, not least because most of the economically important areas had already been colonized or had been integrated into the world economy under the conditions of free trade imperialism. During this era of heightened rivalry, many areas came under the control of one of the great powers for strategic reasons, such as to protect existing imperial interests and communication networks. When existing political regimes or societal orders collapsed in the face of change resulting from global economic integration and European settlement, European powers often absorbed these lands into their empires or intensified the previously loose system of rule. Occasionally, this went hand in hand with military conflict, of which several—above all the South African War (1899–1902)—in turn affected the balance of power on the stage of world politics. It sounds incredible that an entire continent should be partitioned without the consent of its inhabitants, but this is exactly what happened at the Africa Conference in Berlin in 1884. Although Africa was divided up among the European powers on the map, the actual occupation and economic "valorization" did not occur until later. Once the ancient kingdom of Morocco had become a French protectorate in 1912, however, all of Africa (except Ethiopia and Liberia) found itself under European colonial rule.

Of all the countries still free from European control, China was the largest and most economically attractive and was therefore a prime candidate for partition. Yet it did not happen. For one, partition was prevented because more than half a dozen militarily important powers were pursuing overlapping interests and ambitions that were nearly impossible to disentangle geographically. For another, the

Chinese resisted. Their determination to reclaim sovereignty of their country and to make it a powerful nation-state grew in the wake of the xenophobic Boxer Rebellion of 1900, which was crushed by an unprecedented ad hoc coalition of eight interventionist powers who put their rivalries behind them in pursuit of this aim.[21] Following the example set by Japan, the new Chinese nationalist movement now pursued a double strategy of adaptation and resistance.

Not only could territories be divided up, so too could economic opportunities. Of these, the economically and strategically most important were railroad lines, which were always perceived in geostrategic terms. The countries harboring an imperialistic interest in China usually claimed control over a "sphere of influence" alongside a railroad line. In Manchuria entire railroad colonies sprung up under Russian and Japanese control. Starting in 1903 the Trans-Siberian Railroad offered Russia a direct railway line to East Asia, with connections to the Chinese railway network. After 1913 a person could travel by train from Lisbon to Shanghai. Railroad construction was also an excellent business for exporters of heavy industry. However, railroad systems were expensive and technically complex, and they required a great deal of personnel. As of 1920 only 13.2 percent of the world's railroad tracks had been laid in Asia and Africa.[22] The railroad would also never achieve the global omnipresence of the automobile, which had opened up previously impassible regions via cross-country vehicles or trucks by the mid-twentieth century.

The great-powers system of the turn of the century did not become global merely because of the inflated scope of

European ambitions, but also because new centers of power arose. The Spanish-American War of 1898 marked the entrance of the United States onto the stage of world politics. As an industrial producer, the country had already surpassed Britain and Germany. By defeating Spain, the United States received what until then had been the Spanish colony of the Philippines, America's first colonial possession outside the Western Hemisphere. Under the leadership of President McKinley, the United States now acted like a world power, one dependent on open markets abroad for its rapidly developing industry and growing capital wealth and therefore insistent on exerting its influence worldwide. Japan was a far weaker country economically, but since the 1890s it had been a politically independent and militarily significant regional power in East Asia with its own colony (Taiwan) and an informal sphere of influence in Korea. Starting in 1902 it allied itself diplomatically with Britain in a way previously reserved for European powers. Because its own domestic frontier had shifted eastward, Russia joined Britain as a country that was both a great European and Asian power.

Shortly after the turn of the century, all European powers were forced to reduce their ambitions overseas. At first, this had to do with rivalries within Europe: Britain found the German naval buildup increasingly menacing. Therefore, it sought agreements with the United States, France, and Russia, sacrificing territorial claims or informal influence in Latin America, North Africa, and Persia, respectively. Among other things, the negotiations succeeded because these countries shared Britain's growing fear of Germany and were also motivated to make concessions.

The result was the world's first global system of alliances. In addition to "territorialization" and the colonial partitioning of the world, this alliance system was a further example of the "dialectic of globalization and fragmentation."[23] The Russo-Japanese War of 1904–5 also proved a harsh setback to European expansion and demonstrated that world politics was something other than just the European balance of power projected onto a global scale. As the first modern, non-Western military power, Japan defeated the Russian Baltic fleet, which had sailed around Africa to confront them in the decisive sea battle near Tsushima. The Japanese victory was interpreted worldwide as a victory of the modern constitutional state (because Japan had adopted a constitution, formulated with the help of German legal experts, in 1889) over the Russian autocracy and its rather limited mobilization capabilities and as proof that it was possible for non-Western states to emancipate themselves from their dependence on imperialist Europe.

Was the clash of the great powers unavoidable in a world grown so small? What alternatives to this scenario existed? One contrasting trend was that of increasing cooperation in "apolitical" areas of technical and organizational standardization, where international agreements were easily negotiated. As early as 1911 an American legal expert and diplomat published an extensive report taking stock of such developments.[24] Likewise, the old utopian idea of human solidarity received an organizational underpinning for the first time. Henri Dunant, a businessman from Geneva, founded the International Committee of the Red Cross in 1863, which was imbued from the start with a universal, humanitarian aim.[25] Other movements also reached out beyond national borders. The women's suffrage movement united representatives from Europe, North America, New Zealand, Australia, and later India in the fight to gain women the right to vote. In 1893 the World's Parliament of Religions took place for the first time in Chicago.[26] The socialist workers' movement showed its sympathy for colonized peoples by condemning colonial governments for their "excesses," but it stopped short of questioning the system of colonialism and Western predominance as such. In a similar vein, the projects of capitalist internationalism like the American "dollar diplomacy" toward China used economic relations as a means to counter (in this case, Russian and Japanese) strategies of military conquest, while at the same time defending an American interest in the ability to conduct business freely.

Whereas the lack of political influence limited the impact of these private initiatives, the two Hague Peace Conferences (1899 and 1907) did affect a vital aspect of national sovereignty. Very few governments were willing to make the legal commitments proposed there. Still, the principles formulated nearly a century ago on the conduct of war are still valid today. From the very beginning, non-European countries upheld these principles in order to strengthen their claim to an equal standing in the community of nations.[27] All of these internationally oriented alternatives to the power politics of nation-states proved to have one aspect in common, namely, that they were not strong enough to withstand the countervailing forces unleashed in 1914 with the outbreak of World War I. The only exception was the Red Cross.

It would be simplistic to interpret World War I as a direct consequence of the boom in globalization that preceded it. Naturally, the complicated constellation of conflict that existed in the summer of 1914 would have been unthinkable in a general sense without globalization. However, the internal crises of the less globally integrated European regions played a far greater role in starting World War I than did conflicts among the great powers either within Europe or overseas. The genesis of this war was European, but it grew very quickly into a global conflict relying on global resources. The participation of the Ottoman empire (including its Arabian provinces) on the side of the Central Powers, the entry of Japan and particularly the United States into the war, the military campaigns in sub-Saharan Africa, the German attempt to incite the Islamic world, and the deployment of overseas troops in Europe were all globalizing elements.[28] Thus, the year 1914 became a turning point in the national history of many countries located far from the battlegrounds of the "Great War"—such as New Zealand, which lost seventeen thousand soldiers from 1914 to 1918.

On the one hand, World War I represented a phase of convulsively intensified interaction. On the other, numerous long-standing networks were destroyed without being replaced by new, stable structures. Every war damages existing cultural, economic, and human relations and erects barriers between friend and foe. Trade blockades, internment and confiscation, and attacks on communication facilities and shipping became means of warfare. The world's economic division of labor broke down: Europe's industrial export business came to a halt since machines and raw materials were needed for arms production. In the European colonies, Latin America, and China, numerous new industries developed to fill the local demand for what had previously been supplied by the world market. At the same time, many European foreign investments were liquidated in order to finance the war. The monetary system based on the gold standard also broke down, because no state could finance the war without printing more and more paper money.

The war did have an integrating effect within the warring alliances, whose efforts were increasingly coordinated within large political and economic spheres. Several million soldiers from India, Australia, New Zealand, France's African colonies, and—starting in June 1917—the United States were sent to Europe to fight. The colonies supplied Europe with resources such as foodstuffs, machines, and raw materials such as rubber that were vital to the war. To no small degree, it was this ability to mobilize resources on a global scale that enabled the Allies to win.[29] Critical to this success was the protection of maritime supply routes, and the United States eventually entered the war against Germany because American ships had been attacked by German submarines trying to cut off the flow of supplies. The Central Powers lacked access to important resources, particularly to the grain-growing regions in the temperate climate zones overseas.

Unlike weapons, provisions, manpower, and other resources, viruses could cross the front lines without any problem. The microbes of infectious diseases from around the world converged on the battlefields of France and continued to spread. The worldwide flu epidemic of 1918–19 claimed more lives than did the entire war.[30]

1918–1945: Global Crises and Conflicts

World War I ended Europe's domination of the world and shook the international economy to the core. Hardly a soul on earth was not touched in some way by the consequences of the war. The resulting problems were enormous, and because the world would prove incapable of handling all of them, it would eventually have to go through a new world war. In international politics, the prewar order of balancing the power of mighty European nations worldwide had been completely discredited. Initially, a new order of world politics seemed possible, one based on the ideas of democracy, national self-determination, collective security, and free trade outlined in the Fourteen Points of the American president Woodrow Wilson. At the Versailles Peace Conference of 1919, the League of Nations was founded, the first political umbrella organization for the world of nation-states. At the Washington Conference of 1921–22, the first global arms control agreement was signed, in which every naval power, including Japan, agreed on mandatory limitations to the size of their fleets.

After the war, the sovereign nation-state became the standard form of political organization acknowledged around the world. As a result, new states sprang up all over Eurasia from the Baltic to the Balkans all the way to Mesopotamia. The non-Turkish states to emerge from the ruins of the Ottoman empire were first subjected to quasi-colonial control as "mandates" of Britain or France, thus perpetuating in a sense the large colonial empires and regions of informal European rule. However, the war had given great impetus to anticolonial nationalism everywhere. In nearly all colonies, compulsory labor duties and the intensified production of goods essential to the war had increased the burden and impact of colonial rule. Colonial soldiers who had fought on the western front now expected compensation for their sacrifices in the service of the colonial powers. Inspired by a fusion of Western principles of liberty and local desires for autonomy, colonized peoples were demanding self-determination and modernization everywhere. The most conspicuous example of this was India.

Inspired by Wilsonian democratic idealism, anticolonial nationalist movements strove to establish constitutional states without colonial rulers. Soon it became clear that this model of government was competing with two others emerging from the West: Leninism and fascism. The former had obtained a power base as a result of the 1917 Russian Revolution and had established the Communist International (Comintern) for the purpose of propagating the revolution worldwide, a goal that remained far from fulfilled. Attacks against capitalism on its periphery were to be launched in alliance even with the noncommunist forces of the "national bourgeoisies" of these colonies. Moscow became a training center for a young international cadre. Yet the world revolution did not occur, not even in Germany and China, the two countries considered "ripe" for revolution, albeit for different reasons. Hence, no "Soviet bloc" existed before World War II. Under Stalin's leadership, the USSR switched from exporting revolution to "building socialism in one country."

Fascism—we use the term here in a very broad sense to include Mussolini's Italy, National Socialism, and Japanese ultranationalism of the 1930s—had far-reaching imperial ambitions, but unlike communism and liberalism it offered no vision of a social order on a global scale. Fascist ideology was much more eagerly imported by others than exported by its countries of origin. What made fascism attractive in Europe and elsewhere was its combination of national autarkic aims, militarism, statism, and a glorification of technology, which suited the inclinations and interests of military rulers and modernizing autocrats. Both Leninism and fascism were seen as shortcuts to modernity and were eagerly taken up by movements engaged in self-reform or anticolonial resistance.[31]

Fascism did not seek to overcome the "Darwinian" competition among powers for supremacy but applied particularly brutal means in order to succeed at it. In this regard, fascism was a radicalized form of imperialism. It was consistent with their ideology that the fascist regimes systematically disregarded international law and rejected the League of Nations. They viewed the British empire and the immense potential of the United States with jealousy and awe. The only idea the fascists could offer to counter the truly global, liberal concepts of world order for which the leading Anglo-Saxon powers stood was that of the *Großraum*, meaning a large territorial expanse that was dominated politically, militarily, and economically by an imperial power. As a result, this word took on a sinister meaning that has not been shed completely. In the course of World War II, Nazi Germany and Imperial Japan managed to realize their dreams of expansion in Europe and in East and Southeast Asia, respectively, and their *Großräume* became historically unprecedented zones of exploitation and slaughter.

Whereas in the 1880s the economy became politicized, in the years following World War I politics became thoroughly imbued with ideology almost worldwide. Ideological loyalties became detached from the confines of national politics more than before and took on a transnational character. In this regard, something resembling a tripolar civil war was being fought throughout the world between democrats, communists, and fascists.[32] Therefore, occurrences such as the Spanish Civil War or the Chinese Revolution attracted international sympathizers from various political camps.

Despite the universalization of the discourses of nationalism and liberalism, Leninism and fascism, the more conspicuous new feature of the international system was the extraordinary heterogeneity among the nations during the interwar period. Before 1914 the world had primarily consisted of great imperialistic (usually monarchical) powers, smaller states, and the non-Western, more or less dependent periphery. After the war, even among the great powers there was a confusing variety of roles and political systems. Gone was the basic consensus on what constituted "civilized" realpolitik and acceptable deportment that had been worked out over centuries of European diplomatic history. Naturally, realpolitik had never excluded war as a possibility, but the consensus had been reached that the vanquished should not be punished and humiliated too severely. An important novelty in this period was the emergence of more or less independent postcolonial states after decades or even centuries of alien rule: the Irish Free State, the Polish Republic, and Egypt. Austria and Turkey were former centers of empire now stripped of their peripheries. Although quite clear in hindsight, it was not very perceptible at the time that this period represented the decline of the European imperial powers and the rise of the United States as a world power. Politically, the latter remained—at least outside the Western hemisphere—a dormant hegemonic giant, despite its growing economic, financial, and cultural influence.

World War I had destroyed the European power system without replacing it with a global one or even a world government. Europe was losing its influence as the supreme collective power in the world, and neither an American hegemony nor the League of Nations could fill the vacuum. The key concept of the League had been the idea of collective security and the peaceful solution to conflict, yet this concept could not be implemented as long as countries considered any limitation to their national sovereignty unthinkable and the major powers shared neither a vision of a new world order nor the will to act in unison. Japan's invasion of Manchuria in 1931, the Italian attack on Ethiopia in 1936, and Germany's aggressive steps against its neighbors were not countered adequately. Some things had indeed been achieved on the international level: the International Labour Office (ILO), for example, succeeded in improving the working conditions of millions in many countries. Still, the world began to forget that the League was a forum for cooperation and exchange in the tradition of nineteenth-century internationalism and that it was also there to remind the world community of alternative forms of world order.[33]

Following World War I, an attempt was made to reconstruct the global economy as it had existed during the "belle époque" prior to 1914. However, the multilateral interdependence and division of labor of the global economy had been so permanently rocked by the war that it could not be revived.[34] Several structural problems stood in the way of reconstruction. Firstly, all of the warring European nations were severely in debt due to the cost of war, the burden of reconstruction, and, in Germany's case, the reparations it was forced to pay. Only the United States had come out of the war as an important creditor government and exporter of capital. The United States was also earning trade surpluses by exporting its agricultural and industrial products while at the same time protecting its domestic markets with high tariffs. Unlike the debtors of Britain before 1914, the countries in debt to the United States were not able to earn the money they needed to pay back their debts by exporting to America. Soon it became necessary for the global economy to secure a steady flow of American dollars abroad in the form of credit. Still, global capital flows were no longer as large as they had been before 1914.[35]

Secondly, the world markets were suffering from an insurmountable stagnation of demand, and global trade grew much more slowly than did production, a turnaround from the situation of the nineteenth century. During the war the production capacities of heavy industry had been expanded to a point that plants could not be used to capacity during peace time. In agriculture the expansion of arable lands, mechanization, and the growing use of artificial fertilizer had caused increasing overproduction by the mid-1920s; the prices on the world markets had therefore been falling appreciably. Finally, the demand for better-quality consumer goods dropped off everywhere, even in the comparatively wealthy United States.

Thirdly, during the war government authorities everywhere took over the de facto control of production, prices, and currency. Thus, the state became directly responsible for the welfare of its people, the growth of its economy, and social peace. Not only were crises occurring with much greater frequency in the global economy, governments were now expected to react to them. In light of such increasingly costly responsibilities, the political elites attempted to "export" the costs of mediating between domestic interests. Hence, each country began to pursue a "national" economic policy.[36]

Fourthly, the gold standard had been seen as the most important component of the nineteenth-century global economy and as its hallmark. During the war adherence to the gold standard was given up. By the mid-1920s, however, all important currencies were once again linked to gold. In order to defend currency exchange rates and gold reserves, the central banks of the indebted states were forced by the gold standard to maintain a tight money supply and high interest rates, although such a policy severely hampered the growth of the economy and the rate of employment. Those countries with a growing supply of gold, like the United States and for a while France, were unwilling for domestic reasons to accept the consequences, namely, higher domestic prices and increased imports. The gold standard began to function as a crisis mechanism once the United States became the only country to possess sufficient gold reserves, world trade (and therefore foreign exchange earnings) remained weak, and the domestic consequences of monetary policy were taken ever more seriously. The gold standard had thus become "golden fetters."[37]

The bleak fact that the Wall Street crash on 25 October 1929 could develop so rapidly into such an unbelievably large economic crisis worldwide demonstrates that the markets for goods and capital had remained interconnected globally. Numerous factors enabled the crisis to spread to all economies, one after another.[38] The most important of these were the shortage of credit caused by the sudden halt in the export of American capital, the drop in consumer demand, an intensified protectionism, and, finally, the deflationary policies forced upon governments by the gold standard. Attempts to find a solution to the crisis at the international level failed.

Did the Great Depression mean a temporary "end to globalization"? Certainly the international flow of capital did dry up almost completely. Between 1929 and 1935 the volume of world trade also diminished by two-thirds. The slow recovery of business activity after about 1933 was not accompanied by a comparable increase in world trade. International trade and capital transfers were subjected to tight regulation inspired by each country's own national strategy of crisis management and were thereby contained within politically constituted spaces. This was equally true for the American New Deal and its focus on reviving the domestic U.S. market, for the German and Japanese policies of economic recovery through armament and the creation of economically dependent spheres of influence, and for the shift of Britain and France from pursuing worldwide economic integration to strengthening economic ties within each of their colonial empires. The so-called regionalism of the global economy that developed during this period was the result of the primacy given to politics over economic interaction during the crisis.

Although each was motivated by different reasons, the autarky policies of both Germany and Japan in the 1930s and 1940s represented an extreme form of regionalism. These strategies were an effort to create spheres of influence disengaged from the global economy and world politics. With regard to globalization, they meant the coming of a new world war. For several Japanese historians, who speak of World War II as the "fifteen-year war," this new war started in 1931 with the Japanese occupation of Manchuria. With similar justification, it can be argued that the war began with the Japanese invasion of the Chinese mainland in 1937 or with Germany's attack on Poland in 1939.[39] Yet the war did not become truly global until 1941, when the Germans invaded the USSR and the Japanese attacked the United States. As in 1914–18, very little fighting took place in the Western Hemisphere, Australia, and India. However, China, Southeast Asia, and the Pacific did become major battlefields on par with Europe and North Africa. The United States was the only power to be prominently involved in both the Pacific and Atlantic theaters of war, a double role that predestined it to become the leading world power of the postwar period.

The "American Century"

In 1941, when America was still at peace and the Germans and Japanese were in the middle of war, the editor and publisher Henry Luce declared the twentieth century to be the "American Century." This would become an adequate description at least for the second half of the century, thanks to two wars and the particular development of the economy and society in the United States. Without having deliberately sought to attain a leadership role, as early as 1919 the United States found itself in an important position in the global economy and world politics because of its own rapid economic development and Europe's self-destruction.[40] Despite its hesitation to become embroiled in foreign affairs, the United States became extremely influential during the Roaring Twenties not only by way of its capital exports, but also as a social and cultural model. People all over the world saw "America" either with horror or with hope as a vision of their own future.[41]

Mass production, mass consumption, and mass culture are the catchwords that were associated with "Americanism" at the time. The ability of American industry to mass produce standardized goods, the scientific management of Frederick Taylor, and the assembly-line production of Henry Ford fascinated Europe and promised to create surplus profits that would be divided between employee and employer. As the motor of mass production, mass consumption appeared to open the doors to prosperity and social peace.[42] In particular, the mass motorization of the population seemed to represent the big breakthrough. The automobile and the airplane, two new technological inventions to overcome distance that had been given great impetus by World War I, spread throughout the United States faster than in Europe. More controversial than Taylorism and Fordism were the social and cultural changes that were interpreted as being part of the "Americanization" taking place since the late nineteenth century but especially since the 1920s. One such example was the—rather relative—emancipation of women, which succeeded in being as shocking in Berlin as it was in Shanghai; but for young girls in the Weimar Republic and in China, the American "girl" offered an alternative to traditional female role models.

It proved to be much less difficult to spread the products of the American entertainment industry across cultural borders. In the American immigrant society, forms of cultural production had evolved that were easy to commercialize because they made use of idioms intelligible across cultural boundaries and applied the newest technology for recording sound and images. Prior to World War I and within only a few years after the invention of cinematography in 1895, "moving pictures" had spread to every major cultural center of the world, starting in France. Now the products of Hollywood were being exported worldwide. American jazz also proved to be a popular export item and was quickly accepted as a new musical impulse, particularly in Europe, just as European music of late Romanticism found its first enthusiasts in Japan. At first, the Great Depression disappointed the hopes that had arisen in connection with the creation of a society based on mass consumption, and in the growing number of authoritarian regimes, the expansion of American cultural influence was halted. Despite this, many American technologies and forms of production, consumption, and entertainment were adopted even in Nazi Germany.[43] Film industries developed not only in Europe but also in India and Japan.

World War II transformed the United States into the initiator of economic, political, and cultural trends in globalization during the postwar period. The war's influence in this regard was threefold. Firstly, since entering the war in 1941, the United States, under the leadership of Franklin D. Roosevelt, had perceived itself as a world power. It needed to have a voice in determining the world order so as to protect its own national interests, and it could no longer permit regions that were strategically or economically important to fall under the control of enemy nations. Secondly, the war was a highly ideological and racially laden conflict. The political programs of both sides were used to mobilize support and loyalties that cut across national borders: colonial liberation movements supported the colonial masters they had bitterly fought before the war (as in India) or sided with Japan (as in Burma) against the European colonizers. Both collaborators and freedom fighters professed to act in the best interest of their own nations when they took up sides with enemy forces. The German SS recruited people all across Europe who were considered "Nordic." Such a blurring of borders did not create a path toward a new transnational order. Only the program of the victorious Allies, led by the United States, aimed to institutionalize global integration through a comprehensive reconstruction of society, economics, and international relations. Thirdly, the ability of American industry to produce the combat and transportation materials needed by all the Allied forces was a decisive factor leading to the Allied victory.[44] Because it was not directly threatened by military attack, American industry could go an important step further in developing the organization of standardized mass production. Many Europeans and Japanese viewed rationalization, macroeconomic management, internationally integrated mass production, and full employment (as found in the Allied and especially the American war industry) as components of a model they could use to regenerate the economy and society in their own part of the world.

In this sense, the end of the war in 1945 represented a global turning point, not only because it meant the conclusion of a world war that had affected the lives of a greater number of people than any other event in history, but also because it was the will of the victors to create a new world order. The experience of worldwide economic crisis and world war meant that this new agenda would be one of global modernization, spearheaded by the United States.

VI

The golden ages

1945 to the Mid-1970s:
Globalization Split in Two

Political Spaces: Power Blocs, Nation-States, and Transnational Movements

The second postwar period of the twentieth century, known in France as the "thirty glorious years" and in the Anglo-Saxon world as the "golden age," was fundamentally different from the first. It brought about the most comprehensive transformation of economy, society, and culture ever experienced in a period of a few decades. In conjunction with this transformation, numerous new types of integration developed, transnational spaces of interaction were institutionalized, and throughout the world, forms of production and of political organization became increasingly homogeneous. Yet when looking for historical parallels to present-day globalization, historians have tended to turn more often to the period preceding 1914, instead of that following 1945, and have emphasized that post–World War II structures began to disintegrate and mindsets began to change during the course of the 1970s. The second half of the twentieth century started out as a period less influenced by globality than by a variety of overlapping spheres and commitments of a transnational but not a global nature. The great majority of these were the result of political decisions about the acceptable range and intensity of transnational contact and integration.

The most important political structure to evolve during the postwar period was not foreseen in the Allied plans, namely, the partitioning of the world into two ideological blocs competing for power.[1] The creation of these blocs shaped international, transnational, and worldwide integration and the structures of economic and political spheres of interaction. The collapse of Germany and Japan had created large geopolitical power vacuums; but at the same time, the United States and the USSR had attained a definite power advantage over all other countries. Because their respective political and ideological concepts diverged so greatly, it proved difficult for these two power giants to cooperate in order to solve the pressing, inescapable problems of reconstruction and political renewal. As a result, a bipolar geopolitical order was established during 1945–50: Europe was divided by an "iron curtain" and China fell under the control of a communist regime. The Korean War from 1950 to 1953 was essentially a war between the United States and the People's Republic of China that cost both sides many lives yet only ended up confirming the status quo. By then, both superpowers possessed nuclear weapons, and the deployment of these weapons on the battlefield or against the opponent's cities was an important component of each of their military strategies. It took the near catastrophes in Berlin and Cuba (1958, 1962), during which atomic attacks against the enemy were seriously considered, to get both sides to accept coexistence on the basis of mutual deterrence as the state of normalcy in international affairs.[2] Deterrence was "indivisible" and therefore global. Its instruments consisted of intercontinental rockets, radar- and satellite-based air surveillance, and fleets of missile-armed nuclear submarines patrolling under the surface of the earth's oceans. In essence, deterrence was the threat to annihilate life on earth.

Direct military confrontation between the superpowers could now only be expected as a result of some existential threat (or an error in their early warning defense systems), and this situation eventually helped erode the blocs. The American leadership was horrified by the possible scenarios described in the domino theory, in which one client regime after another would fall under communist influence or control. For this reason, the United States felt compelled to defend anticommunist South Vietnam militarily against the communist North. One indication of the erosion within the blocs was that the United States found little support for this war among its allies, despite its reassurances, inspired by the domino theory, that Berlin was actually being defended on the Mekong. Therefore, in the late 1960s the U.S. government decided to switch from maintaining a bipolar system to cultivating a multipolar one instead. With an eye on the nineteenth-century system of great powers, it attempted to counterbalance the USSR with China.

The creation of political blocs also affected other levels of political organization. The Soviet sphere of influence was primarily a military security zone in which the Stalinist system of society and economy was gradually established. The relationship that developed between the Soviet

Union and its allies is best described as a traditionally hegemonic one. It revealed the structural deficits of the USSR that made this "incomplete superpower" competitive only militarily.[3] China and Yugoslavia played special roles because they had loosened themselves from the grip of the USSR but remained communist regimes. While Yugoslavia worked to develop contacts throughout the world, China almost completely isolated itself from the rest of the world in the 1960s.

In the West, the consequences of bloc-building were far more complex because the United States was not satisfied with creating merely a security zone. It pursued the threefold aim of containing communism, securing and institutionalizing an open, capitalist global economy, and pacifying Western Europe, which meant integrating (West) Germany. The only conceivable means to achieve this threefold aim was to coordinate economically prosperous, politically stable nation-states. The effect of this comprehensive agenda actually countered global integration because it gave priority to the internal reorganization of the "West" over any compromise with the USSR and therefore encouraged bloc-building. At the same time, it encouraged deeper integration within the Western bloc.[4] Defense was the only area organized in a hegemonic manner under the leadership of the United States. Otherwise, there developed an associative multilateralism in which the individual nation-states retained a considerable amount of political leeway. This is evident particularly in the process of European integration, which the United States supported but which was pursued and shaped by the Europeans themselves. The creation of the European

Coal and Steel Community (1952) and the European Economic Community (1957) were two of the first steps toward plucking certain areas from the realm of national sovereignty and putting them under the jurisdiction of "supranational" bodies. This led to a thoroughly new, continually transforming political organization situated somewhere on a scale between a federation of states and a federal state.[5] Within the framework of the Council of Europe, human rights cases could be brought for the very first time before a supranational court. In addition, the countries of the Western bloc belonged to numerous economic organizations, which institutionalized cooperation among themselves and limited the actual autonomy of the national governments but not their legal sovereignty.

This multilateralism and European integration in particular have been described as processes limiting the power of nation-states, and indeed, many of the pioneers of the European idea did envision their goal as the incorporation of these various countries into a "United States of Europe." However, European unification was also a project that European nation-states pursued for their own interests. In fact, economic and political cooperation within a framework of European structures may even have been necessary for the survival of the nation-state model.[6] In its "mature phase," the new European nation-state was based on a broad consensus, first, that economic liberalism in its purest theoretical form had been discredited by the Great Depression and the ambitions of aggressive nationalism had finally been dashed by World War II, and second, that "the West" had to join together to repel the threat posed by the "Soviet empire." Historical experience and fears circulating at the time prompted compromises within states and between them, which turned the reinvigorated European nation-state into a forum for mediating between the needs of domestic societal stability and international integration. When theorists speak of "postinternational politics," they are referring to the numerous multilateral economic and political integrations that were only possible in this postwar context.[7]

The European state was also a postimperial state. After the war ended, the colonial empires of the victorious Allied powers did not survive for long. Britain granted India and Pakistan their independence in 1947, once it became clear that Britain's resources, already badly drained by the war, were insufficient to secure militarily its rule in Asia while upholding its status as both a great power and a welfare state. Burma and Ceylon also soon set out on their own, and the Netherlands gave up its Indonesian colonial empire. As the Cold War intensified, the United States—although previously hostile to colonialism—began to view European colonial rule as a bulwark against communism and to see colonial markets as important factors for the economic stability of their European allies. Therefore, they supported the French in the war in Indochina against the communist movement for national independence. The strategy failed with the defeat of the French in 1954 at Dien Bien Phu; as a consequence, Vietnam was divided in two and the French retreated from Asia. The old imperial order and the new Cold War order coexisted only briefly. In 1956 the United States and the USSR worked together to end the French-British-Israeli intervention against Egypt, which was demanding its independence and a leadership role in the region. The United States now deemed it necessary to stop its allies from squandering the resources needed for the defense of Europe and from driving liberation movements throughout the world into the arms of communism. It supported decolonialization and guaranteed economic aid for those new states that chose to ally themselves with the "right" side. In the shadow of the Suez Crisis and the Algerian War (1954–62), the chances for success of colonial independence movements improved dramatically. In the early 1960s the colonial empires quickly collapsed to the point that only a few possessions remained.

The retreat of the colonial rulers did not reintroduce the *status quo ante* of local political institutions, traditional modes of economic production, and cultural patterns, but led instead to the emergence of nation-states embedded in a global economy and world politics. In 1950 there were 81 nations on earth; in 1960, 90 nations; in 1970, 134 nations.[8] The majority of the new states found it impossible to fulfill the expectations placed on a sovereign nation-state. This is one reason why a dubious political innovation of the twentieth century—military dictatorship—rapidly spread during this era of decolonialization and Cold War. The new states shared a number of common interests, especially the need to overcome their "underdevelopment" and the desire not to be lorded over by the world's two major power blocs. This aim expressed itself in the movement of bloc-free nations, in the efforts to organize Afro-Asian solidarity, and in the demand for foreign aid and a more just world order. Still, the Third World was also divided over contradictory interests. Moreover, the bitter lesson that political sovereignty did not automatically mean true autonomy and that the economic dependence on the First World continued to exist strengthened those who spoke out in favor of policies pursuing autarky and sovereignty. In short, the Third World did *not* become a sphere of supranational political integration and cooperation.[9]

Non-European nations found they could voice their positions particularly well in the United Nations, where they soon represented the majority of the membership. The UN had been founded in 1946 in San Francisco by fifty countries as the successor to the League of Nations.[10] Originally, it was to become the key body of a postwar order established by the Allied powers and endowed with a certain amount of legal authority. The emergence of the political blocs in the East and West prevented this. As a result of the Soviet boycott of the UN, the organization became an almost exclusively Western forum for a while. At the end of the 1950s, the nations of the "global south" succeeded in getting UN debates to focus on the topics of underdevelopment and the struggle against colonialism and thereby alerted the world to these issues. The position taken by the UN General Assembly also helped discredit French colonial rule in Algeria—even among France's allies.[11]

The United Nations institutionalized principles such as the concept of national self-determination and sovereignty and the idea of inalienable human rights, thus turning these potentially contradictory principles into political resources accessible to all. The rights and duties of sovereign nations were increasingly defined within the framework of the United Nations. In a world dominated by the existence of major political blocs, however, the definition of such rights and duties became primarily a means of propaganda, and the degree to which nations complied with these was always measured with a double standard.

Following World War II, transnational political solidarity continued to play an important role in international politics. This was fostered by the commonalities shared among the nations within each of the Cold War blocs, by the colonial independence movements, and finally, by the protest movements of the late 1960s. Moreover, the "domestic policies" of nation-states were increasingly dominated by supranational agendas and trends, which in turn standardized political interests worldwide. Whereas the transnational, anticommunist, intellectual milieu of the 1950s and the solidarity within the colonial independence movements were elitist phenomena within a supranational sphere of discourse, the societal basis for transnational politicization was substantially broadened by the student-led protest movements of the 1960s. This also demonstrates the particularly close connection between international transformation and domestic social change during the Cold War. The issues taken up by the protest movements can only be fully understood once the economic and sociocultural transformations of this period are taken into consideration.

The Institutions of the Global Economy

From 1948 to 1958 the global economy grew on average by 5.1 percent annually; growth increased to 6.6 percent annually in the period between 1958 and 1970. Simultaneously, world trade increased faster than production (for the first time since 1914): in these two periods it grew by an average of 6.2 percent and 8.3 percent, respectively.[12] The "big boom" was also a boom in globalization in many respects, because it intensified the intercontinental movement of capital, goods, and people and was closely linked to the institutional framework of the global economy.

According to the concepts of the Allies, the new political order for the world, as represented by the UN, was to be accompanied by a new economic order. In 1944 they agreed at the Bretton Woods conference on the basic principles of a legal and institutional framework for a free global economy. Above all, this framework was to prevent countries from combating economic problems unilaterally, that is, by limiting the movement of goods and capital, as had been done in the interwar period. The idea was to ensure that international cooperation remained compatible with full employment policy. For this purpose, institutions were created that still influence economic globalization today: the World Bank (actually the International Bank for Reconstruction and Development, or IBRD) was to offer credit for reconstruction and long-term economic modernization; the International Monetary Fund (IMF) was to create a system of fixed exchange rates and assist member states with short-term problems in their balance of payments; and the General Agreement on Tariffs and Trade (GATT) was to offer a forum for negotiating comprehensive tariff cuts. Unlike its policy following World War I, the United States forgave the debts of its allies, but it expected that the protective tariff systems established in the 1930s, particularly the British empire tariffs, would be repealed so as to benefit free world trade.

Postwar economic planning failed even faster than political planning did. Still, within the West (meaning North America, Western Europe, Japan, and Australia) a new region of economic multilateralism emerged. This development is interesting in four different respects. First, a new global division of labor was prevented from evolving on its own because Europe's economy was ruined by the war and the United States held a supremely powerful position. Within the context of the escalating confrontation with the Soviet Union, the United States decided in 1947 to shoulder the costs of a major reconstruction program, even if this would become far more expensive than originally planned and meant deferring the principles of Bretton Woods. The result was the Marshall Plan, which helped Europeans finance reconstruction and socially stabilizing consumption and (perhaps even more importantly) forced them to cooperate with one another.[13] "Free peoples" elsewhere in the world also received American aid.

Second, although the institutions set up at the Bretton Woods conference never truly worked in the way they had been planned, the principles on which they were based remained the reference point for economic policy-making and provided the impetus for an increasingly lively economic exchange in the "West." However, these principles were only applied gradually and never entirely. The processes of currency convertibility and trade liberalization were curtailed whenever individual countries felt this was necessary for reasons of domestic stability and for protecting their autonomy in economic policy-making. Often, a partial liberalization in a smaller context was established instead of the strict implementation of the Bretton Woods principles, as was the case with the European Payments Union and the European Economic Community. The scope and intensity of trade and capital relations thus remained below the level of 1913. It was not possible to create structures for an economic division of labor on a global scale in areas, for example, that were shielded by the protectionist agricultural policy of the EEC.

Third, the Cold War caused the political elites of the Western countries to see themselves as dependent on one another. The need to integrate weaker partners into the U.S.-dominated system went unquestioned, and the United States retained a willingness to compromise. The same held true for the political dynamics within each country, where competition between the Eastern and Western "systems" provided an incentive for elites to agree to redistributive social and economic policies. On the whole, this increased the acceptance of existing economic arrangements in the world. At least this was true of prospering Europe. But the Bretton Woods system also had its more or less forcefully integrated periphery, namely, the military dictatorships and autocracies supported by the United States and in part established through military intervention in Latin America and Asia.

Fourth, the generally optimistic climate of an era when mere reconstruction quickly turned into unprecedented growth was important. In the late 1950s the United States experienced its first negative balance of trade and payments in a long time, a fact illustrating that the Europeans had caught up with America and signaling that the global economy had stabilized. This growth also legitimated the international economic order. At the same time, the forces encouraging growth—from the Marshall Plan to increasing levels of trade, technological transfer, and the mechanisms of payment balances—were themselves international in nature.

The—desired—dynamics of global economic integration (in connection with the expensive, worldwide political involvement of the United States) soon put an end to the Bretton Woods system. In 1961, just as the free convertibility of Western currencies had become an important element of the Bretton Woods order, the American dollar found itself under pressure: its value could only be upheld by a series of emergency measures such as capital controls, intervention on the part of the European central banks, and trade restrictions. Faced with the choice of either cutting back public expenditure or giving up the defense of the dollar's rate of exchange, the Nixon administration decided in 1971 on the latter and took the dollar off the gold standard. The exchange rates were reset in international negotiations but were then set free completely soon afterward.

The three basic principles of Bretton Woods were fixed exchange rates, the free flow of goods and capital, and the freedom of governments to implement their economic policies. Taken together, these three principles were not compatible. In the final analysis, the internal contradictions of the Bretton Woods system were what caused it to fail. These contradictions were revealed by the "holes in the system" that enabled globalization outside of the channels institutionalized by the state, especially the private market for gold, used for speculating against the dollar, and the so-called Eurodollar market. This market was comprised of the dollars earned in business transactions outside of the United States that were deposited in European (primarily London) banks and then loaned out from these banks. This capital evaded all government attempts to control interest rates, money supply, and capital flows. These are the origins of today's unregulated capital markets.

Most other channels of global economic integration remained under the control of tighter government regulation. The development of capital markets is best compared with that of the shipping business, in which flags-of-convenience countries offered shipping companies a similarly unregulated basis for their operations worldwide, despite the more tangible nature of the business. Still, the shipping business was only one sector in the increasingly perfected land-sea system. With the introduction of innovations such as pipelines and containers, the business became even more efficient, on the one hand, while becoming more territorially anchored, on the other. Government regulation was more obvious in civil aviation. This industry developed rapidly in the 1950s, particularly after the first commercially successful jetliners were introduced (the Boeing 707 in 1958). Transcontinental flights became a common occurrence, and a global system of airports and air traffic control was set up. Airline companies often were—and in most cases still are today—enterprises not managed according to principles of a market economy but highly subsidized prestige projects that operated on protected markets. Just as obvious is state influence in the area of postal and telecommunications infrastructure, where state-run enterprises enjoyed a near monopoly until the 1990s.

The capabilities of the state to intervene are reflected even in the activity of multinational corporations. Private enterprises belong to the most successful and stable organizations transcending national borders.[14] The development of a global economy in the nineteenth century was primarily the result of private business initiative. Back then, the first multinational companies were established in which production was vertically integrated, from obtaining the necessary raw materials to marketing the final product. Another type of multinational company dated back to the protectionism of the 1880s. In order to surmount tariff walls and produce directly in protected markets, companies established plants abroad that were small copies of the original company using its technological and organizational know-how. Understandably, this type of international business activity blossomed in the interwar climate of economic fragmentation, but it remained the dominant form even after 1945. At first, this was because Europeans could not afford the imported goods that had to be paid in dollars; later, the tariffs imposed by the "Common Market" encouraged American companies to build production plants in Europe. Not until the end of the 1960s did European and Japanese firms also set up comparable structures. The activities of multinational companies thus were influenced by the regulations on tariffs and transfers. Yet, at the same time, multinational firms could secure a great deal of leeway by internalizing the flow of goods and money, and the foreign profits of American multinational corporations were the sources of the Eurodollar markets.[15] Naturally, multinational corporations could also influence political decisions directly in smaller, poorer states whose entire economic production was smaller than that of a large company. Today's multinationals, which organize global production networks by allocating each of the various steps of production to the place where it can be performed the cheapest, are the result of the liberalization of the product and capital markets since the 1970s.

Shipping, trade, telecommunication, air travel, and the activities of international firms tied together global networks that extended beyond the world of Bretton Woods to include the Third World and the Soviet sphere of influence. They did not include China, though, which was pursuing a course of economic, political, and cultural autarky. Still, the intensity of economic integration in the Second World of communism and the Third World of postcolonial states was not as great as that of the First World. The countries fully integrated into the global economy were the oil-producing nations of the Near and Middle East. The percentage of the worldwide oil supply produced by these nations became greater the more the importance of coal declined and the more the rise of the automobile made petroleum an indispensable resource.[16] Otherwise, the predominant economic policy implemented by non-Western countries was one based on the Soviet model of the interwar period, in which rapid industrialization through central economic planning was given utmost priority and only very selective ties to the global economy existed. Until the mid-1960s, when the "transfer ruble" and a bank for international settlements were established, only bilateral trade relations were conducted in the communist world, which was organized economically in the Council for Mutual Economic Assistance (COMECON). The attempt to coordinate national economic plans within the framework of the COMECON and to organize a division of labor among the national economies failed in the mid-1950s because of the resistance put up by many countries that did not want to have their economic specialization imposed upon them from outside.

The majority of Third World countries also followed a strategy of industrialization that remained decoupled from the global economy, because this global economy was considered responsible for their underdevelopment. The world market seemed to be a synonym for incalculable fluctuations in demand, crushing competition, and financial dependency. It was thought that rapid development could be brought about through a process of centrally planned industrialization in which resources were concentrated in a few key industries and in import substitution, meaning the domestic production of certain goods instead of their importation. It was essential for this policy that unregulated transnational integration be prohibited. The foreign aid given these countries starting in the 1950s was also integrated into this strategy—this was one of the concessions inspired by Cold War competition between the superpowers. Whereas import-substituting industrialization, as undertaken in Latin America and India, was initially successful, it soon ran up against the problems of small domestic markets and rigid systems of bureaucracy and clientele politics. The East Asian variation was more successful. Here, planners used the nearly 150-year-old concept of protection for "infant industries" developed by Friedrich List by systematically nurturing industries viable on the world market and pressuring them to export quickly.[17] This approach was an imitation of Japan, which had risen to the ranks of a first-class industrial power by the 1960s. By this time, the cautious beginnings of a comparable development were already noticeable in Taiwan and South Korea, Hong Kong and Singapore. The difference between these countries and others in the developing world was that they managed to transform economic growth into a stable increase in per capita income. Elsewhere in the Third Word, population growth devoured most of economic growth.

Sociocultural Globalization?

In the social theories of the 1950s, it became popular to envision modernization as creating an increasingly integrated and homogenous world. A distinction was made between traditional, nonindustrial communities and modern, industrialized, complexly differentiated societies. A normal path of social development was postulated to exist that would lead countries from one condition to the other and thus culminate in worldwide modernity. Poor, nonindustrialized societies were described as "developing countries" that still had several stages to go through on this prescribed path toward becoming industrialized nation-states. Independent of their ideology or specific societal systems, developed societies appeared to exhibit the common trends of economic growth, bureaucratization, and an increasingly complex social organization. This is why it was soon argued that we were witnessing the "end of ideology" and a convergence of systems.[18]

However, social development in the 1950s was predominantly one of disentanglement rather than globalization. The mass migration taking place in the postwar period led to ethnic partitioning in central Europe as much as in Israel or British India, from which Islamic Pakistan was hastily separated at the point of independence. In Europe, societies became more homogeneous than ever before in the modern era.[19] In everyday life, the big wide world loomed especially large in the geostrategic fear of "the Russians" (for those in the West) or of a nuclear war (for everyone). People did not have the money to travel abroad, and the horizons of their world were usually defined by the problems of organizing their daily lives. In the early 1950s Americans were still most likely to leave their continent as members of the large armed forces deployed all over the world, especially in Western Europe, Korea, and Japan. The impression these military forces (and the increasing number of American tourists) left on the population of the host country was almost certainly much bigger than vice versa. This interaction has been described as a massive though involuntary cultural exchange program: while the soldiers and their families lived in a world of their own on military bases throughout the world, they also brought with them the first examples of American mass culture and consumption patterns to populations still struggling to overcome the cultural and economic disruption caused by the war.

Nevertheless, the early development of mass consumption and the mass media is not primarily a story of globalization. The development of a consumer society in Europe in the 1950s has been described as cultural Americanization. Indeed, prosperity first meant that it became possible for Europeans to emulate American consumption patterns, notably by purchasing consumer goods already common in the United States, such as automobiles, refrigerators, and television sets. However, this behavior was often accompanied by a hostile attitude toward social Americanization. The European television programming broadcast in the 1950s bore little resemblance to the American.[20] Mass consumption and mass media had an integrating effect initially on the national level, despite the obvious function of the United States as a role model. Only in certain specific milieus did people tend to consume demonstratively the products of the American entertainment industry—first jazz, then certain movies, and finally rock 'n' roll—in order to distance themselves from established norms and assert subcultural identities.[21]

Starting in the 1960s a series of interconnected trends in sociocultural globalization could be observed. For one, the frequency of personal contact between people from different continents increased. The European economic miracle led first to full employment and then to the employment of foreign labor. During the period of decolonialization, many people migrated from the colonies to the motherlands—a reversal of the flow of migration that had taken place for centuries from Europe out into the world. European and American metropolises became multicultural centers that were more closely linked to their immediate vicinities, the homelands of the immigrants, and the centers of the global economy than they were to the nation-states in which they were located.[22] Similar megacities evolved in other places on the planet. Only in the communist world did effective restrictions on the freedom of movement and on participation in the global economy limit the experience of globalization.

As Europeans and Americans became more and more well off, they began to spend their vacations abroad and soon had charter flights whisk them away to even more distant paradises. The possibility that packaged vacations could act as forms of cultural exchange was rather small, but the travel industry did integrate a series of regions into the global economy. "Pleasure peripheries" sprang up around the industrialized regions of the world, and soon jobs and tax income in these areas became dependent on the flow of tourists. The effort to maintain this tourism affected foreign policy priorities and changed the social character of these tourist areas, which sought to present themselves as intact havens far from the modern world. Often a bit of the supposedly traditional local color was created specifically to comply with the presumed taste of the vacationing guests.[23]

The globalization of mass production, mass consumption, and mass media was the explicit aim of the visions of the future inspired by modernization theory, and growth was the common denominator of major social projects in the West, the East, and the Third World. Unlike industrialization, the global homogenization of consumption desires and cultural references, oriented on the standards of industrial civilization, advanced rapidly in the 1960s and increasingly transcended the borders of nations and political power blocs. In light of the economic lead enjoyed by the United States, it is no surprise that the postwar pioneers in this area were globally marketed American products: Coca-Cola became a global brand during World War II. (McDonald's has only been in business outside of North America since 1971.)[24] Television, movies, advertising, and contacts with relatives in the Western capitals of the world helped Western consumption goods or local products modeled after them (plastic sandals, jeans, T-shirts) become commonplace nearly everywhere. The United States, the wealthiest, most powerful, and furthest developed society on earth, was also the reference point of individual consumption desires and collective efforts at modernization—be it in the USSR, the Third World, or France. Everywhere the aim was to take up the "American challenge," to meet American power head on, and to be able to offer one's own citizens the same standard of living as Americans. Consumer societies developed not only in the Western world, but also somewhat later in communist Eastern Europe and in enclaves of the Third World.

Evidence of such a homogenization of consumption patterns and attitudes could be found far beyond America's political sphere of influence, namely, the capitalist "free world." Did this mean the entire planet was being Westernized or even Americanized? This would be too simplified an interpretation. Indeed, given the hegemonic position of the United States, it seems paradoxical that the cultural, social, and economic changes inspired and often encouraged by Washington, Detroit, or Hollywood did not result in others imitating a "U.S. model." There are three reasons why such imitation did not occur. First, multinational corporations, usually American ones, brought new products and tastes to Europe, Latin America, and Asia, but new methods of enterprise organization had to be thoroughly adapted to local conditions if they were to be introduced at all, and macroeconomic institutions exhibited an even greater path dependency (meaning the resistance to change induced by the weight of past decisions, the rigidity of basic social structures, and political traditions). Therefore, even when we speak of the West, we do not talk about Americanization but still refer to the numerous national and regional "varieties of capitalism" and to the selective adaptation and "innovative hybridization" of specific American models in European and Japanese industry.[25] Second, the United States has produced various, often contradictory sociocultural patterns (a fact that contributed significantly to the global success of American cultural production). Moreover, the United States and the West have themselves changed during the process of cultural globalization. In the 1960s pop music burst forth from "America" to embrace the entire globe. Although American in origin, it was not considered socially acceptable even there at first and only managed to spread throughout the world because it was taken up by London art students hungry for authenticity, on the one hand, and by American teenagers with a great deal of purchasing power, on the other. Throughout its journey, pop music continued—in the East and West—to express resentment against the Establishment before it finally found a home in the—global—mainstream. Similar processes can also be observed in industry. Third, the superficial Westernization of world culture and the spread of industrial mass production often occurred indirectly and via detours and always remained dependent on mediators from the recipient or third-party countries. They could only occur in places where people creatively adapted new importations to the local context in a way that promised them social, cultural, or economic advantages. The conflict between what was one's "own" and what was the "other" coming from another civilization has always been one between the "old" and the "new" *within* a civilization as well. Americanization, even under conditions of U.S. hegemony, involved bargains struck with, and within, the societies it affected.

The blessings of global modernity did not go unchallenged. Where these blessings were bestowed upon the industrialized West, they were also accompanied by demands for sweeping emancipation and postmaterialist lifestyles, demands that found a voice in the protest movements of the 1960s. In the communist world, where industrialization was organized by authoritarian states, demands for freedom were expressed in movements like the "Prague Spring." In the Third World it appeared necessary to find a fundamental alternative to the paradigm of progress, which remained apparently unattainable using either the Western-capitalist or the Soviet model. Although the protest movements of the 1960s may well have focused on numerous issues of only local significance, these protesters also saw themselves reacting to the increasing homogenization of the world as marked by consumption and growth and implemented by the means of state repression.[26]

In three major ways the Vietnam War, which escalated in 1965 when American troops were deployed there, helped to coalesce what had been rather diffuse and localized demands and to establish contact among protesters. Firstly, the war offered emancipation movements all over the world not only a common enemy in the form of "U.S. imperialism and capitalism" but also new mentors and models. The Cultural Revolution initiated by Mao Zedong and the revolutionary activism of Che Guevara were alternative revolutionary enactments that appeared to thrive without authoritarian bureaucracy and the corrupting effects of consumer society. Thus, for a brief moment in history, the constant, centuries-old flow of political ideas from Europe to other continents was reversed. After being almost completely isolated from the world and barely affected by the sociocultural movements of the 1960s, China was now exerting a considerable influence on political agendas throughout the rest of the world.[27] Yet, even in this episode of cultural transfer, we again find that this influence was integrated elsewhere in ways ranging from creative adaptation to complete misunderstanding.

Second, the Vietnam War took place in full view of the world population, thanks to relatively uncensored television reporting. Unlike earlier wars, this one was not only highly visible but equally visible everywhere. Media theorists began to claim that the world had become a global village with a single common horizon. Third, the television images of the war had a demoralizing impact on the American public, although this impact has been overestimated. What is significant is that the mainstream media of the postwar economic boom, such as television and radio broadcasting, could influence public opinion in a manner contrary to the interests of the Establishment that controlled it. American-inspired popular music became the symbolic expression of protest against the politics of the American establishment worldwide, not the least in the United States itself. Pop music in the 1960s became an international medium of expression, one that was a globally marketed consumer good and a resource for protest against capitalist society.

It is also a result of the 1960s protest culture that the influence of humankind on the natural environment throughout the world became a political issue. In the twenty-five years from 1950 to 1975, the world population grew from 2.5 billion to 4 billion. For the first time, people began to wake up to the fact that the earth was being perceptibly altered by human activity, specifically by economic growth and the population explosion—for example, not until the twentieth century had humans ever had a greater influence on the earth's atmosphere than have microbes. Because environmental damage and pollution were caused locally, they were perceived for a long time strictly as local phenomena. Even though it had already been known in the 1860s that British emissions made their way to Scandinavia, not for another century did the problem become a political issue. Since the 1960s the global climate has been discussed as a global phenomenon, and an important turning point came with the Conference on the Causes of Climate Change that took place in Boulder, Colorado, in 1965.[28] At this conference the vulnerability of the environment and the finiteness of the earth's resources available for production and consumption were debated widely and extensively as political issues for the first time. Earth Day 1970, when 20 million Americans demonstrated against the rape of nature, and the report

published by the Club of Rome in 1972[29] mark a significant change in the environmental consciousness of the
general public. People were now aware that life on earth
was threatened not only by the possibility of abrupt annihilation through nuclear war but also by the creeping
destruction of the planet through the exploitation of its
resources and environmental pollution.

Conclusion

A New Millennium

Since the end of the 1960s, the postwar structures outlined in the preceding chapter have been changing. This change marks the beginning of the most recent phase of globalization, which is widely believed to be the first real globalization and which receives the most attention from the social sciences. From the perspective of (contemporary) history, six aspects need to be considered.

First, the most important developments in international politics since the 1970s were the erosion and eventual collapse of the USSR and the Soviet bloc. When these fell apart, so did the global power structure established by the Cold War, namely, the "bipolar" international system. It is not yet exactly clear what new structures will evolve in a world order marked by American claims to leadership. The military interventions into Afghanistan and Iraq in 2002 and 2003 have not clarified the outlines of this new order. Indisputably, the United States is the only superpower in the world. But the inescapable leadership role it assumes in world politics and the global economy also brings with it special responsibilities and challenges. At the same time, the means of classic power politics are of little use in dealing with many of the policy issues and actors who are currently playing a greater role in world politics than they had previously. Examples range from regulating global capital markets to fighting transnational terrorism. By the end of the twentieth century, the entire world was affected by "postinternational" multilateralism, which arose in the West and had worldwide consequences following the first Conference on Security and Cooperation in Europe (1973–75) where human rights, culture, and the environment were discussed in close connection with international security. Such "interdependency issues"—human rights, the global climate, free world trade, and so on—became increasingly important and were addressed within the framework of international organizations and "regimes." The number of international agreements on these topics continues to grow, as does the number of nongovernmental actors involved in international politics. Such actors include not only respectable organizations like Greenpeace and Amnesty International but also their illegal and immoral counterparts, namely, the networks of organized crime and political terrorism. What these new actors on the stage of world politics and the nations of the world have in common is that they think in global terms when it comes to addressing problems and their solutions.

Second, the 1970s also witnessed the onset of the crisis facing the welfare state and its interventionist economic policies designed to secure full employment and stable growth. This crisis is often thought to be a consequence of globalization, but it is also an important cause of the new thrust in the globalization process. The policies of liberalization, privatization, and tax cuts, as first introduced in Britain after 1979, created the conditions necessary for "spontaneous" economic globalization—that is, for the emergence of global spheres of interaction in which government regulation was minimal. Once state socialism collapsed in the eastern half of Eurasia and after the People's Republic of China abandoned its policy of state-supported subsistence as guaranteed by the "iron rice bowl," the quasi-autarkic system of bureaucratic planning and provisioning for all aspects of daily life disappeared.

Third, the liberalization of international exchange was followed by a period of rapid expansion and intensification in international trade and finance. In 1986, after the "big bang" of deregulation in the City of London, one of the world's financial capitals, financial markets began to develop extraordinarily quickly. This was compounded by two qualitative changes. The first of these was the transformation of centrally managed and globally dispersed multinational corporations into transnational firms, whose national affiliation became even more difficult to ascertain. These firms represent a form of global economic organization that is hierarchical in structure rather than set up as a network and governed by markets. The other qualitative change was the growth in the emerging economies, particularly the East Asian "tigers." These countries developed into industrial economies at an intermediate level of technology often by integrating themselves into the production chains of transnational corporations. Thus, not only did the communist Second World fall apart, so did the Third World of developing countries. Of these, several rose to the same level of prosperity as the

West and Japan, whereas for many others there can be no talk of any sort of development.

Fourth, the advances in communications and data-processing technology were decisive factors enabling financial markets to boom worldwide, transnational corporations to set up their global organizations, and the "Asian tigers" to emerge as major producers in the computer and computer chip industries. Since the mid-1990s the Internet has become generally accessible on a strictly private, "noncentered" basis. Yet it is more of a metaphor than a cause for the integration that has taken place as a result of data processing and electronic media.[1] At the same time, not all parts of the world have been integrated into the electronic network; in fact, a "digital gap" has developed between those with access to computer network capabilities and those without.

Fifth, the electronic media has been a particularly powerful catalyst in popularizing the interconnectedness of our world and encouraging reflection on it. Everywhere, material and cultural "goods" from other continents are being marketed aggressively and made available for either creative adaptation or unreflected consumption. It remains to be seen just how much cultural Americanization, aided by the global predominance of the English language, will be balanced out by other sources and different paths of cultural transfer. Even if the West today is less culturally influenced by Japan, for example, than it was around 1880 at the height of Japanism in the visual arts, quite a few trends in fashion, design, and theory that enjoy worldwide popularity are created in Italy or France. Throughout the world, transnational corporations are faced with the challenge of taking local peculiarities of the market into consideration.

In the second half of the twentieth century, more and more people began to think in a global context. Still, this context provides a primary identification for only a few "free-floating" groups, found primarily among internationally oriented elites and, on the low end of the economic scale, among economic refugees who have been forced to migrate. Midway between these two extremes, other groups are gradually emerging, such as religious diaspora communities that are establishing contact with one another worldwide.[2]

Sixth, as integration intensifies around the world, it enables and facilitates not only legal transfers but also illegal ones in the drug trade, money laundering, the smuggling of refugees, and new forms of the slave trade. Often, illegal transfers are linked at important junctures to the legal global economy: the financial capitals of the West are populated by highly paid specialists with international backgrounds, as well as by illegal migrants who provide services, such as cheap childcare, on which the economic output of many well-qualified employees, including the highly "globalized" elites, depends. As a rule, it is merely a person's political and ideological standpoint that determines which of these illegal networks are seen as nothing more than the result of unjustifiably strict legislation and which are abhorred as social evils to be combated at all costs.[3]

On the Road to a Global Age?

All this adds up to a new thrust in globalization. The widely held opinion that we are living in the "age of globalization" is well founded. However, is this truly a new age? Does it differ from all its historical predecessors by exhibiting a quantitatively and qualitatively new type of globality? If there is indeed a turning point at which globalization becomes a central feature of history and of many human experiences, then it occurred in the early modern period of discovery, slave trade, and "ecological imperialism," not in the late twentieth century. Another thrust in globalization took place in the wake of the industrialization of transportation and communication starting in the mid-nineteenth century. Globalization influenced the lives of the majority of humankind already at the end of the nineteenth century and became part of the personal experience of a much broader section of the population following World War II. In the twentieth century human experience was influenced particularly by the experience of (economic) world crises, world wars, and the possibility of immediate or gradual world annihilation. The degree of economic exchange that existed in 1913 was not achieved again until the 1970s, and in some areas, the year 1913 has not yet been surpassed.[4] One of the most compelling descriptions of global capitalism is still that found in *The Communist Manifesto*, written in 1848 by Karl Marx and Friedrich Engels.[5] When globalization again accelerated in the 1980s and 1990s, globality no longer was anything particularly special.

Throughout history supranational networks and permeable borders were the norm. The European nation-state of the nineteenth and twentieth centuries, which has tacitly served as the starting point in most analyses of globalization, is a comparatively recent exception. Rarely in history have entire economies deliberately isolated themselves thoroughly from the outside world. Precursors of the fashionable and successful "network companies" with internalized markets even existed in the trading empires of the early modern period. Our point is not that it is possible to compare our times directly with those of the seventeenth or eighteenth centuries, but that the patterns argued to be so characteristic for the current age of globality were actually present in earlier times.

It is difficult to find any empirical evidence to support the more extravagant analyses of present-day globalization offered by some theorists. In many cases, these analyses are more accurately described as predictions or depictions of utopias, positive as well as negative ones. The following examples may illustrate this point.

1. *Global social structures.* The earth we inhabit is one large enclosed arena. Its vastness has offered humankind generations of opportunities, while its finiteness has placed limits on what we can do. This world is not yet filled with social structures that could be considered global; it still contains a variety of overlapping networks of interaction, whose actual working is often more obscured than illuminated by subordinating them under the broad heading of "globalization." The North Atlantic region together with Japan constitute—as they did a century ago—a zone of particularly dense interaction, while the Pacific region, hindered by the major economic crisis to hit Asia in 1997, is on its way to becoming such a zone. Enclaves of globalization exist outside of the West. One example is the export economy

that has developed in the Pearl River delta in southern China. The Chinese companies located here are
far more closely involved with the numerous
transnational corporations that produce goods in
this region than they are with one another or
with the Chinese economy as such.[6] In other parts
of the world, people and countries find themselves
dependent on worldwide networks but often not in
a position to participate to their own advantage.
This is particularly true for Africa, which constitutes
no more than a blank space on the map of globalization when considering legal trade relations only.[7]
This is due in good part to the dysfunctional
structures that are kept alive through international
arms trade, transfers of resources, and foreign aid.

2. *Does globalization mean the end of the nation-state?* So
far, no Western country has succeeded in drastically
reducing the portion of the national income admin-
istered and distributed by the state. In fact, those
countries most intensively involved in global interaction are also the ones with the highest ratio of
government expenditure to GNP. Furthermore, tariff
and trade "wars" are certainly not things of the past,
and governments worldwide are very active in con-
trolling and restricting international migration.
Even the dismantling of government regulations
should not be regarded as evidence of the impend-
ing "end of the nation-state." On the contrary, to
take government out of the economy was, at least
for Margaret Thatcher, a necessary step in order to
strengthen Britain as a nation-state.[8]

3. *Globalization as Americanization.* "Globalization" is
   one chapter in the history of the "rise of the West."
   From the onset, networks have not been peaceful,
   voluntary interdependencies. At the same time, it
   would be incorrect simply to equate globalization
   with steamrollering Westernization or Americanization. Over and over again, we find evidence revealing
   the phenomenon of creative adaptation, in which
   "foreign" solutions are often selected (and modified
   in the transition) on the basis of rational considera-
   tions and because they represent preformulated
   answers to questions and problems that have already
   been solved elsewhere. Most innovations imported
   from America serve as means employed for local
   purposes or as molds to be filled with local content.
   Transformation inspired and encouraged by
   Americans, or more generally, by the West does
   not automatically imply Americanization or
   Westernization, chiefly because all processes of
   cultural or institutional transfer, diffusion, and
   cross-fertilization require a substantial amount of
   local cooperation and adaptation, which results
   in the transformation en route of what is being
   transferred.
4. *The transformation of space and time.* Today it takes
   less time and money to travel than it has ever taken
   before. Borders are easier to cross, and to "exit" one
   country for another is an option available to more
   and more individuals and firms.[9] Still, it is not
   unimportant where a person *is*. Locality remains a
   matter of fate. There is a world of difference between

people who are voluntarily mobile and people who have been forced on the move. The claim that geographical space has been replaced by "space of flows" may border on cynicism. But it is correct that spaces are created more through networking than vice versa. Even in earlier eras of simpler means of transportation, natural barriers—oceans, mountains, deserts—rarely proved to be insurmountable obstacles when there was a will to expand, explore, and establish contact with distant lands.

Globalization: Putting the Concept into Perspective

Globalization, like "modernization" and other multidimensional concepts, is not easy to quantify. We can only speak to a very limited degree about "more" or "less" globalization. The various processes summarized under the general rubric of globalization do not always occur concurrently or lead in the same direction. Time and again throughout modern history, economic integration and political deglobalization have occurred simultaneously. Time and again, military and imperial expansionism has gone hand in hand with a diminishing curiosity about the cultures of other civilizations. Processes that fragment our world, such as ethnic cleansings in which certain population groups are singled out and persecuted, produce refugee migrations worldwide and create new diasporas in the countries willing to take them in. For its part, the United Nations ensures the existence of nation-states and defends the principle of nonintervention, on the one hand, but institutionalizes values, such as human rights, that undermine national sovereignty, on the other.

"Globalization" is closely linked to "modernization." Even in the premodern era, structured connections over long distances existed in the world. But not until the advent of the cultural creativity that developed within European modernity—summed up by keywords like rationality, organization, industry, and communications technology—were such connections able to attain a new range and intensity. At the same time, European modernity developed from the very beginning within a global context. Asia, the Islamic world of the Near East, later the two Americas, Africa, and the South Seas all became reference points for Europe's self-enhancing definition of itself as a universal civilization. Once these areas of the world had been traveled, colonized, and interwoven into the fabric of world trade, they responded to the impulses of modernization emanating from Europe and North America via the transmission paths of globalization by assimilating and reworking them, and produced—with various degrees of determination and success—variations of their own: multiple modernities.[10]

It makes sense to use "globalization" as a generic term referring to a number of explicitly describable structures and interactions with a planetary range. Globalization should not be thought of as an autonomous process, an unstoppable historical movement, and an imperative political necessity. When using such an encompassing term, we must take particular care not to reify globalization and must repeatedly insist that macroprocesses always be interpreted as the result of individual or collective action.

Global connections are forged, maintained, reshaped, and destroyed by nation-states, companies, groups, and individuals. They are the object of conflicts of interest and politics. They even out differences and create new ones; they produce winners and losers.[11] The same is true for the *destruction* of global structures. Globalization is propagated by people harboring a variety of visions and strategies. We must remember that much of what appears in retrospect to have been the logical consequence of a world growing smaller was also due to unintended side effects of behavior that definitely had no global aims. The worldwide Spanish flu epidemic and the founding of the League of Nations both occurred in 1919, and both had consequences for globalization. Yet the "actions" causing each of these events were not at all similar.

The term "globalization" evens out such differences. If we use it with some critical awareness, we should be able to avoid oversimplification and reification. Such caution, however, is always required when dealing with the grand categories with which historians also sometimes work. In the terminological repertoire of historical analysis, "globalization" will take its place alongside "industrialization," "urbanization," or "democratization." This does not mean that the topic of "globalization" will necessarily become less politically controversial. Most likely, "globalization" will maintain its polemic power, much as "capitalism" and "imperialism" have. The fact that historians assert with calm detachment that this phenomenon has existed for a long time does not preclude the need to make a political assessment of its impact on the present.

Notes

CHAPTER I

1. Jan Aart Scholte, *Globalization: A Critical Introduction* (Basingstoke and New York: Palgrave, 2000).

2. See Hans van der Loo and Willem van Reijen, *Modernisierung. Projekt und Paradox* (Munich: Deutscher Taschenbuch Verlag, 1992), p. 242.

3. For references to the most important works by the authors being mentioned in the following, see the list of recommended literature.

4. Susan Strange, *The Retreat of the State: The Diffusion of Power in the World Economy* (Cambridge: Cambridge University Press, 1996).

5. Unrivaled in any Western language is the historical analysis of Wolfgang Reinhard, *Geschichte der Staatsgewalt. Eine vergleichende Verfassungsgeschichte Europas von den Anfängen bis zur Gegenwart* (Munich: C. H. Beck Verlag, 1999), pp. 509–36.

6. There is a huge body of literature on the various concepts of "culture." As convenient introductions, see John R. Hall, Mary Jo Neitz, and Marshall Battani, *Sociology on Culture* (London and New York: Routledge, 2003); Adam Kuper, *Culture: The Anthropologists' Account* (Cambridge, Mass.: Harvard University Press, 1999).

7. Roland Robertson, *Globalization: Social Theory and Global Culture* (London: Sage, 1992), p. 100; id., "Glocalization: Time-Space and Homogeneity-Heterogeneity," in *Global Modernities*, Mike Featherstone, Scott Lash, and Roland Robertson, eds. (London: Sage, 1995), pp. 25–44.

8. See Robert J. C. Young, *Colonial Desire: Hybridity in Theory, Culture, and Race* (London: Routledge, 1995), pp. 18–28.

9. David Harvey, *The Condition of Postmodernity: An Enquiry into the Origins of Cultural Change* (Oxford: Blackwell, 1989), esp. p. 240.

10. Scholte, *Globalization*, pp. 46–50.

11. For a critical analysis of this concept, see Justin Rosenberg, *The Follies of Globalisation Theory* (London: Verso, 2000).

CHAPTER II

1. See Friedrich H. Tenbruck, "Gesellschaftsgeschichte oder Weltgeschichte?" *Kölner Zeitschrift für Soziologie und Sozialpsychologie* 41 (1989): 417–39.

2. Ulrich Beck, *What Is Globalization?* (Cambridge: Polity Press, 2000), p. 23f.

3. Bernhard Harms, *Volkswirtschaft und Weltwirtschaft. Versuch der Begründung einer Weltwirtschaftslehre* (Jena: Fischer Verlag, 1912); Michael D. Bordo, Alan M. Taylor, and Jeffrey G. Williamson, eds., *Globalization in Historical Perspective* (Chicago: University of Chicago Press, 2003).

4. A magisterial summary of present-day knowledge is the work by Dirk Hoerder, *Cultures in Contact: World Migrations in the Second Millennium* (Durham, N.C.: Duke University Press, 2002); see also Robin Cohen, ed., *The Cambridge Survey of World Migration* (Cambridge: Cambridge University Press, 1995).

5. See Robin Cohen, *Global Diasporas: An Introduction* (London: UCL Press, 1997).

6. There are numerous overviews of this topic. See Herbert S. Klein, *The Atlantic Slave Trade* (Cambridge: Cambridge University Press, 1999); Ira Berlin, *Generations of Captivity: A History of African-American Slaves* (Cambridge, Mass.: Belknap Press, 2003).

7. Barry Buzan and Richard Little, *International Systems in World History: Remaking the Study of International Relations* (Oxford: Oxford University Press, 2000). For a programmatic treatment, see Thomas Bender, ed., *Rethinking American History in a Global Age* (Berkeley, Los Angeles, and London: University of California Press, 2002).

8. Examples include Frank Ninkovich, *Modernity and Power: A History of the Domino Theory* (Chicago: University of Chicago Press, 1994), and Emily S. Rosenberg, *Financial Missionaries to the World: The Politics and Culture of Dollar Diplomacy, 1900–1930* (Cambridge, Mass.: Harvard University Press, 1999).

9. A. G. Hopkins, "Back to the Future: From National History to Imperial History," *Past & Present* 164 (1999): 198–243; Linda Colley, "What Is Imperial History Now?" in *What Is History Now?* David Cannadine, ed. (Basingstoke: Macmillan, 2002), pp. 132–47.

10. See Stephen Howe, *Empire: A Very Short Introduction* (Oxford: Oxford University Press, 2002); Susan E. Alcock, Carla M. Sinopoli, Terence N. D'Altroy, and Kathleen D. Morrison, eds., *Empires: Perspectives from Archaeology and History* (Cambridge: Cambridge University Press, 2001).

11. A founding text for the "new colonial history" is Frederick Cooper and Ann Laura Stoler, eds., *Tensions of Empire: Colonial Cultures in a Bourgeois World* (Berkeley, Los Angeles, and London: University of California Press, 1997). For a more traditional approach, see Jürgen Osterhammel, *Colonialism: A Theoretical Overview*, 2d ed. (Princeton, N.J.: Markus Wiener, 2005).

12. Still among the best outlines of the field is Michael Geyer and Charles Bright, "World History in a Global Age," *American Historical Review* 100 (1995): 1034–60.

13. Patrick Manning, *Navigating World History: Historians Create a Global Past* (New York: Palgrave, 2003), p. 15.

14. See a similar treatment with a different emphasis: Bruce Mazlish, "Comparing Global History to World History," *Journal of Interdisciplinary History* 28 (1998): 385–95.

15. According to David S. Landes, *The Wealth and Poverty of Nations: Why Some Are So Rich and Some So Poor* (New York: W. W. Norton, 1998).

16. See Jürgen Osterhammel, *Geschichtswissenschaft jenseits des Nationalstaats. Studien zu Beziehungsgeschichte und Zivilisationsvergleich* (Göttingen: Vandenhoeck & Ruprecht, 2001), ch. 7; Philip Pomper, Richard H. Elphick, and Richard T. Vann, eds., *World History: Ideologies, Structures, and Identities* (Oxford: Blackwell, 1998).

17. See the journal *Review,* published since 1978. To date, Immanuel Wallerstein's major work comprises three volumes: *The Modern World-System I: Capitalist Agriculture and the Origins of the European World Economy in the Sixteenth Century* (New York: Academic Press, 1974); *The Modern World-System II: Mercantilism and the Consolidation of the European World Economy, 1600–1750* (New York: Academic Press, 1980); *The Modern World-System III: The Second Era of*

Great Expansion of the Capitalist World-Economy, 1730–1840s (San Diego: Academic Press, 1989).

18. On the various analytical aspects of "incorporation," see Thomas D. Hall, "The World-System in Perspective: A Small Sample from a Large Universe," in *Globalization: Critical Concepts in Sociology*, 6 vols., Roland Robertson and Kathleen E. White, eds. (London and New York: Routledge, 2003), 1: 361–64.

19. As an introduction, see Immanuel Wallerstein, *The Essential Wallerstein* (New York: New Press, 2000).

20. Niklas Luhmann, *Die Gesellschaft der Gesellschaft* (2 vols., Frankfurt a.M.: Suhrkamp, 1997), 1: 145–71. This work, which has not yet been translated into English, is the magnum opus of the leading (German) theorist of *Weltgesellschaft* or "world society."

21. See Fredrik Barth, "Towards Greater Naturalism in Conceptualizing Societies," in *Conceptualizing Society*, Adam Kuper, ed. (London: Routledge, 1992), pp. 17–33; Ulf Hannerz, *Transnational Connections: Culture, People, Places* (London: Routledge, 1996), pp. 34–56; John Obert Voll, "Islam As a Special World-System," in *Journal of World History* 5:2 (1994): 213–26.

22. Paul Arndt, *Deutschlands Stellung in der Weltwirtschaft* (Leipzig: Teubner, 1913), pp. 1–4.

23. Manuel Castells, "Materials for an Exploratory Theory of the Network Society," *British Journal of Sociology* 51 (2000): 5–24.

24. John W. Burton, *World Society* (Cambridge: Cambridge University Press, 1972), pp. 35–51.

25. See Göran Therborn, "Globalizations: Dimensions, Historical Waves, Regional Effects, Normative Governance," *International Sociology* 15 (2000): 151–79.

26. See also Hermann Lübbe, "Netzverdichtung. Zur Philosophie industriegesellschaftlicher Entwicklungen," *Zeitschrift für philosophische Forschung* 50 (1996): pp. 133–150.

27. Gary Gereffi and Miguel Korzeniewicz, eds., *Commodity Chains and Global Capitalism* (Westport, Conn.: Praeger, 1994).

28. Klaus J. Bade, *Migration in European History* (Oxford: Blackwell, 2003), p. 39.

29. Alfred W. Crosby, *Ecological Imperialism: The Biological Expansion of Europe, 900–1900* (Cambridge: Cambridge University Press, 1986).

30. M. Panić, *Globalization and National Economic Welfare* (Basingstoke: Macmillan, 2003), pp. 4–5, differentiates between "spontaneous," uncoordinated globalization and "institutionalized" globalization.

31. Roland Robertson and Kathleen E. White, "Globalization: An Overview," in Robertson and White, *Globalization*, 1: 1–44, here p. 8.

Chapter III

1. See André Gunder Frank and Barry K. Gills, eds., *The World System: Five Hundred Years or Five Thousand?* (London: Routledge, 1993).

2. William H. McNeill, the eminent world historian, has defined the term "ecumene" very broadly. We revert to its original reference to religious solidarity.

3. Michael McCormick, *Origins of the European Economy: Communications and Commerce, A.D. 300–900* (Cambridge: Cambridge University Press, 2001).

4. Luigi Luca Cavalli-Sforza et al., *The History and Geography of Human Genes* (Princeton: Princeton University Press, 1994).

5. Jacques Gernet, *A History of Chinese Civilization*, 2d ed., trans. J. R. Foster and Charles Hartman (Cambridge: Cambridge University Press, 1999), pp. 287–88.

6. See Frances Wood, *The Silk Road: Two Thousand Years in the Heart of Asia* (London: British Library, 2003).

7. See Thomas T. Allsen, *Culture and Conquest in Mongol Eurasia* (Cambridge: Cambridge University Press, 2001).

8. Janet Abu-Lughod, *Before European Hegemony: The World System, A.D. 1250–1350* (New York and Oxford: Oxford University Press, 1989); Robert Bartlett, *The Making of Europe: Conquest, Civilisation, and Cultural Change, 950–1350* (Harmondsworth: Penguin, 1994); Michael Mitterauer, *Warum Europa? Mittelalterliche Grundlagen eines Sonderwegs* (Munich: C. H. Beck Verlag, 2003), pp. 199–234.

9. William H. McNeill, *Plagues and Peoples* (Harmondsworth: Penguin, 1979), pp. 141–85.

10. See John Lee, "Trade and Economy in Preindustrial East Asia, c. 1500–c. 1800: East Asia in the Age of Global Integration," *Journal of Asian Studies* 58 (1999): 2–26.

11. Victor Lieberman, ed., *Beyond Binary Histories: Re-imagining Eurasia to c. 1830* (Ann Arbor: University of Michigan Press, 1999).

12. Jeremy Black, *War and the World: Military Power and the Fate of Continents, 1450–2000* (New Haven, Conn., and London: Yale University Press, 1998), pp. 30–32.

13. William H. McNeill, "The Age of Gunpowder Empires, 1450–1800," in *Islamic and European Expansion: The Forging of a Global Order*, Michael Adas, ed. (Philadelphia, Penn.: Temple University Press, 1993), pp. 103–39.

14. See the attempt to describe the advance of the white man in North America from the perspective of the Native Americans in Daniel K. Richter, *Facing East from Indian Country: A Native History of Early America* (Cambridge, Mass.: Harvard University Press, 2001).

15. Richard White, *"It's Your Misfortune and None of My Own": A History of the American West* (Norman, Okla.: University of Oklahoma Press, 1991), pp. 18–24.

16. For a depiction of the history leading up to this development, see Barry Cunliffe, *Facing the Ocean: The Atlantic and Its Peoples, 8000 BC–AD 1500* (Oxford: Oxford University Press, 2001).

17. Robin Blackburn, *The Making of New World Slavery: From the Baroque to the Modern* (London: Verso, 1997), chs. 4, 8, 9.

18. Philip D. Curtin, *The Rise and Fall of the Plantation Complex* (Cambridge: Cambridge University Press, 1990).

19. J. K. Thornton, *Warfare in Atlantic Africa, 1500–1800* (London: UCL Press, 1999), p. 62.

20. Klein, *Atlantic Slave Trade*, p. 211 (table A.2.).

21. Dennis O. Flynn, "Born with a 'Silver Spoon': The Origin of World Trade in 1571," *Journal of World History* 6 (1995): 201–21.

22. Ramon H. Myers and Yeh-chien Wang, "Economic Developments, 1644–1800," in *The Cambridge History of China*, Willard J. Peterson, ed., vol. 9, pt. 1 (Cambridge: Cambridge University Press, 2002), p. 590.

23. Fernand Braudel, *Civilization and Capitalism, 15th–18th Century*, 3 vols. (London: Collins, 1981), esp. vol. 2; R. J. Barendse, *The Arabian Seas: The Indian Ocean World of the Seventeenth Century* (Armonk: M. E. Sharpe, 2002), pp. 152–96.

24. Patrick K. O'Brien, "European Economic Development: The Contribution of the Periphery," *Economic History Review* 35 (1982): 1–18.

25. See John E. Wills, Jr., "European Consumption of Asian Production in the 17th and 18th Centuries," in *Consumption and the World of Goods*, John Brewer and Roy Porter, eds. (London: Routledge, 1993), pp. 133–47; Sidney W. Mintz, *Sweetness and Power: The Place of Sugar in Modern History* (New York: Viking, 1985); William Gervase Clarence-Smith, *Cocoa and Chocolate, 1765–1914* (London and New York: Routledge, 2000).

26. See as a huge inventory of this knowledge Donald F. Lach, *Asia in the Making of Europe*, 3 vols. in 9 parts (vol. 3 with Edwin J. Van Kley) (Chicago and London: University of Chicago Press, 1965–93).

27. Arnold Hottinger, *Akbar der Große (1542–1605). Herrscher über Indien durch Versöhnung der Religionen* (Munich: Fink, 1998), pp. 123–39.

28. On the transfer of scientific knowledge and technology from Europe to East Asia, see Shigeru Nakayama, *Academic and Scientific Traditions in China, Japan, and the West* (Tokyo: University of Tokyo Press, 1984).

29. Quoted in P. J. Marshall and Glyndwr Williams, *The Great Map of Mankind: British Perceptions of the World in the Age of Enlightenment* (London: Dent, 1982), p. 1.

30. On the early stage, see Donald Keene, *The Japanese Discovery of Europe, 1720–1830*, rev. ed. (Stanford: Stanford University Press, 1969); on the later period, see Douglas R. Howland, *Translating the West: Language and Political Reason in Nineteenth-Century Japan* (Honolulu: University of Hawaii Press, 2002).

Chapter IV

1. See Heinz Gollwitzer, *Geschichte des weltpolitischen Denkens*, vol. 1, *Vom Zeitalter der Entdeckungen bis zum Beginn des Imperialismus* (Göttingen: Vandenhoeck & Ruprecht, 1972), pp. 212–22.

2. Bruce Lenman, "Colonial Wars and Imperial Instability, 1688–1793," in *The Oxford History of the British Empire*, vol. 2, *The Eighteenth Century*, ed. P. J. Marshall (Oxford: Oxford University Press, 1998), pp. 159–63.

3. See Peggy Liss, *Atlantic Empires: The Network of Trade and Revolution, 1713–1826* (Baltimore and London: Johns Hopkins University Press, 1983). On the revolutionary "underworld" of the Atlantic, see

Peter Linebaugh and Marcus Rediker, *The Many-Headed Hydra: Sailors, Slaves, Commoners, and the Hidden History of the Revolutionary Atlantic* (Boston: Beacon Press, 2000).

4. See J. Klaits and M. H. Haltzel, eds., *The Global Ramifications of the French Revolution* (Cambridge: Cambridge University Press, 1994).

5. Sidney Pollard, "Industrialization, 1740 to the Present," in *An Historical Geography of Europe*, Robin A. Butlin and Richard A. Dodgshon, eds. (Oxford: Clarendon Press, 1998), pp. 280–99; Peter N. Stearns, *The Industrial Revolution in World History* (Boulder, Colo.: Westview Press, 1993); Mikuláš Teich and Roy Porter, eds., *The Industrial Revolution in National Context* (Cambridge: Cambridge University Press, 1996).

6. Jan de Vries, "The Industrial Revolution and the Industrious Revolution," *Journal of Economic History* 54, no. 2 (1994): 249–70; C. A. Bayly, *The Birth of the Modern World, 1780–1914: Global Connections and Comparisons* (Oxford: Blackwell, 2004), pp. 58–83.

7. Ralph Davis, *The Industrial Revolution and British Overseas Trade* (Leicester: Leicester University Press, 1979), p. 15, table 2.

8. Joseph E. Inikori, *Africans and the Industrial Revolution in England: A Study in International Trade and Economic Development* (Cambridge: Cambridge University Press, 2002).

9. François Crouzet, *A History of the European Economy, 1000–2000* (Charlottesville: University of Virginia Press, 2001), p. 117.

10. James E. Vance, *Capturing the Horizon: The Historical Geography of Transportation Since the Sixteenth Century* (Baltimore and London: Johns Hopkins University Press, 1990).

11. See Asa Briggs and Peter Burke, *A Social History of the Media: From Gutenberg to the Internet* (Cambridge: Polity Press, 2002), pp. 133–43.

12. Peter J. Hugill, *Global Communications Since 1844: Geopolitics and Technology* (Baltimore and London: Johns Hopkins University Press, 1999), pp. 25–53.

13. Daniel R. Headrick, *When Information Came of Age: Technologies of Knowledge in the Age of Reason and Revolution* (Oxford: Oxford University Press, 2000), pp. 189–93.

14. For the enormous importance of free trade as a creed of the age, see Anthony Howe, *Free Trade and Liberal England* (Oxford: Clarendon Press, 1997).

15. Paul Bairoch, *Economics and World History: Myths and Paradoxes* (New York: Harvester Wheatsheaf, 1993), pp. 38–41.

16. The concept was developed by Ronald Robinson and John R. Gallagher, "The Imperialism of Free Trade," *Economic History Review* 6 (1953): 1–15.

17. The Ottoman empire was the first non-Western government to launch policies of reform. This is a central motive in a short but excellent book by Roderic H. Davison and Clement Dodd, *Turkey: A Short History*, 3d ed. (Huntington: University of Texas Press, 1998).

18. See Donald Read, *The Power of News: The History of Reuters, 1849–1989* (Oxford: Oxford University Press, 1992).

19. For an up-to-date introduction to the history of Christian missions, see various chapters in Adrian Hastings, ed., *A World History of Christianity* (London: Cassell, 1999).

20. See David Crystal, *English As a Global Language* (Cambridge: Cambridge University Press, 1997), pp. 24–63.

21. Manuel Castells, *The Information Age*, vol. 1, *The Rise of the Network Society* (Malden, Mass.: Blackwell, 1996), 92.

22. See Tom Standage, *The Victorian Internet: The Remarkable Story of the Telegraph and the Nineteenth Century's On-Line Pioneers* (London: Weidenfeld & Nicolson, 1998).

23. Bade, *Migration in European History*, p. 40.

24. Wolfram Fischer, "Wirtschaft und Gesellschaft Europas 1850–1914," in *Handbuch der europäischen Wirtschafts- und Sozialgeschichte*, ed. id., vol. 5 (Stuttgart: Klett-Cotta, 1985), pp. 31, 35.

25. Seymour Drescher and Stanley L. Engerman, eds., *A Historical Guide to World Slavery* (New York: Oxford University Press, 1998), p. 387. In addition, the Arab-organized "oriental slave trade" shipped at least 1.7 million people between 1820 and 1877 alone from East Africa to North Africa and Arabia and across the Indian Ocean (ibid., p. 43).

26. Albert G. Kenwood and Alan L. Lougheed, *The Growth of the International Economy, 1820–2000: An Introductory Text*, 4th ed. (London: Routledge, 1999), p. 78.

27. Christine Dobbin, *Asian Entrepreneurial Minorities: Conjoint Communities in the Making of the World Economy, 1570–1940* (Richmond, UK: Curzon, 1996); Claude Markovits, *The Global World of Indian Merchants, 1750–1947: Traders of Sind from Bukhara to Panama* (Cambridge: Cambridge University Press, 2000).

28. C. Knick Harley, "Transportation, the World Wheat Trade, and the Kuznets Cycle, 1850–1913," *Explorations in Economic History* 17 (1980): 218–50; Sidney Pollard and Paul Robertson, *The British Shipbuilding Industry, 1870–1914* (Cambridge, Mass.: Harvard University Press, 1979), pp. 9–24.

29. Kevin H. O'Rourke and Jeffrey G. Williamson, *Globalization and History: The Evolution of a Nineteenth-Century Atlantic Economy* (Cambridge, Mass.: MIT Press, 1999).

30. William Arthur Lewis, *Growth and Fluctuations, 1870–1913* (London: Allen and Unwin, 1978).

CHAPTER V

1. David Vincent, *The Rise of Mass Literacy: Reading and Writing in Modern Europe* (Cambridge: Polity Press, 2000), pp. 10–11.

2. See Natascha Vittinghoff, *Die Anfänge des Journalismus in China (1860–1911)* (Wiesbaden: Harrassowitz, 2002); Ami Ayalon, "Political Journalism and Its Audience in Egypt, 1875–1914," *Culture & History* 16 (1997): 100–121.

3. Stephen Kern, *The Culture of Time and Space, 1880–1918* (London: Weidenfeld & Nicolson, 1983), p. 2.

4. Clark Blaise, *Time Lord: Sir Sandford Fleming and the Creation of Standard Time* (London: Weidenfeld & Nicolson, 2000).

5. David S. Landes, *Revolution in Time: Clocks and the Making of the Modern World* (Cambridge, Mass.: Harvard University Press, 1983), p. 287.

6. Michael Williams, *Deforesting the Earth: From Prehistory to Global Crisis* (Chicago and London: University of Chicago Press, 2003), pp. 384–85.

7. August Sartorius von Waltershausen, *Die Entstehung der Weltwirtschaft. Geschichte des zwischenstaatlichen Wirtschaftslebens vom letzten Viertel des 18. Jahrhunderts bis 1914* (Jena: Gustav Fischer Verlag, 1931), p. 10.

8. John Dunning, *Multinational Enterprises and the Global Economy* (Wokingham: Addison-Wesley, 1993); Mira Wilkins, ed., *The Growth of Multinationals* (Aldershot: Edward Elgar, 1991).

9. Wolfram Fischer, *Expansion, Integration, Globalisierung. Studien zur Geschichte der Weltwirtschaft* (Göttingen: Vandenhoeck & Ruprecht, 1998), pp. 37–48.

10. Francis S. L. Lyons, *Internationalism in Europe, 1815–1914* (Leiden: Sythoff, 1963); Martin H. Geyer and Johannes Paulmann, eds., *The Mechanics of Internationalism: Culture, Society, and Politics from the 1840s to the First World War* (Oxford: Oxford University Press, 2001).

11. William C. McNeill, "Money and Economic Change," in *The Columbia History of the Twentieth Century*, Richard W. Bulliet, ed. (New York: Columbia University Press, 1998), pp. 283–313; Barry Eichengreen, *Globalizing Capital: A History of the International Monetary System* (Princeton, N.J.: Princeton University Press, 1996).

12. John H. Drabble, *An Economic History of Malaysia, c. 1800–1990: The Transition to Modern Economic Growth* (Basingstoke: Macmillan, 2000), ch. 4.

13. See Frederick S. Weaver, *Latin America in the World Economy: Mercantile Colonialism to Global Capitalism* (Boulder, Colo.: Westview Press, 2000).

14. Angus Maddison, *The World Economy: A Millennial Perspective* (Paris: OECD, 2001), p. 126, table 3-1b.

15. Aristide R. Zolberg, "Global Movements, Global Walls: Responses to Migrations, 1885–1925," in *Global History and Migrations*, Wang Gungwu, ed. (Boulder, Colo.: Westview Press, 1997), pp. 279–307.

16. Antoni Estevadeordal, Brian Frantz, and Alan M. Taylor, "The Rise and Fall of World Trade, 1870–1939," NBER Working Paper 9318, Washington, D.C., 2002.

17. Charles S. Maier, "Consigning the Twentieth Century to History: Alternative Narratives for the Modern Era," *American Historical Review* 105 (2000): 807–31; Knut Borchardt. *Globalisierung in historischer Perspektive* (Munich: Bayerische Akademie der Wissenschaften, 2001).

18. Maddison, *The World Economy*, p. 242, table B-11.

19. Walter Nugent, *Into the West: The Story of Its People* (New York: Knopf, 1999), p. 131.

20. Bouda Etemad, *La possession du monde: Poids et mesures de la colonisation (XVIIIᵉ–XXᵉ siècles)* (Brussels: Éditions complexes, 2000), p. 175, table 13.

21. See Lanxin Xiang, *The Origins of the Boxer War: A Multinational Study* (London: Routledge-Curzon, 2003).

22. William Woodruff, *Impact of Western Man: A Study of Europe's Role in the World Economy, 1750–1960* (New York: St. Martin's Press, 1966), p. 253, table VI/1.

23. Ian Clark, *Globalization and Fragmentation: International Relations in the Twentieth Century* (Oxford: Oxford University Press, 1997), p. 33ff.

24. Paul Reinsch, *Public International Unions: Their Work and Organization. A Study in International Administrative Law* (Boston: Ginn, 1911).

25. Caroline Moorehead, *Dunant's Dream: War, Switzerland, and the History of the Red Cross* (London: HarperCollins, 1998).

26. See Richard Hughes Seager, *The World's Parliament of Religions: The East/West Encounter, Chicago, 1893* (Bloomington, Ind.: Indiana University Press, 1995).

27. Jost Dülffer, *Regeln gegen den Krieg. Die Haager Friedenskonferenzen 1899 und 1907 in der internationalen Politik* (Frankfurt a.M.: Ullstein, 1981).

28. Hew Strachan, *The First World War*, vol. 1, *To Arms* (Oxford: Oxford University Press, 2001); Gerd Hardach, *The First World War, 1914–1918* (Berkeley, Los Angeles, and London: University of California Press, 1981), ch. 9.

29. See Avner Offer, *The First World War: An Agrarian Interpretation* (Oxford: Oxford University Press, 1989).

30. Gina Kolata, *Flu: The Story of the Great Influenza Pandemic of 1918 and the Search for the Virus That Caused It* (London: Macmillan, 1999).

31. Theodore H. von Laue, *The World Revolution of Westernization: The Twentieth Century in Global Perspective* (Oxford: Oxford University Press, 1987), pp. 5, 99–147.

32. Eric J. Hobsbawm, *The Age of Extremes: A History of the World, 1914–1991* (New York: Pantheon, 1995), p. 144.

33. See F. S. Northedge, *The League of Nations: Its Life and Times, 1920–1946* (Leicester: Leicester University Press, 1986).

34. For a contemporary's analysis, see John Maynard Keynes, *The Economic Consequences of the Peace* (London: Macmillan, 1919), ch. 2 and 6.

35. Derek H. Aldcroft, *The European Economy, 1914–1990*, 3d ed. (London: Routledge, 1993), pp. 57–62.

36. Harold James, *The End of Globalization: Lessons from the Great Depression* (Cambridge, Mass.: Harvard University Press, 2001), p. 117.

37. Barry Eichengreen, *Golden Fetters: The Gold Standard and the Great Depression, 1919–1939* (Oxford: Oxford University Press, 1992); Patricia Clavin, *The Great Depression in Europe, 1929–1939* (Basingstoke: Macmillan, 2000), pp. 61–67.

38. See Dietmar Rothermund, *The Global Impact of the Great Depression, 1929–1939* (London and New York: Routledge, 1996).

39. See D. Cohen, "Historiography, War, and War Crimes: The Representation of World War II," *Rechtshistorisches Journal* 19 (2000): 413–31.

40. Donald Reynolds, "American Globalism: Mass, Motion, and the Multiplier Effect," in *Globalization in World History*, A. G. Hopkins, ed. (London: Pimlico, 2002), pp. 243–60.

41. Richard F. Kuisel, *Seducing the French: The Dilemma of Americanization* (Berkeley, Los Angeles, and London: University of California Press, 1993).

42. D. A. Hounshell, *From the American System to Mass Production, 1800–1932: The Development of Manufacturing Technology in the United States* (Baltimore: Johns Hopkins University Press, 1984).

43. Philipp Gassert, *Amerika im Dritten Reich. Ideologie, Propaganda und Volksmeinung 1933–1945* (Stuttgart: Franz Steiner Verlag, 1997); Michael H. Kater, *Different Drummers: Jazz in the Culture of Nazi Germany* (New York and Oxford: Oxford University Press, 1992).

44. See Richard Overy, *Why the Allies Won* (New York and London: W. W. Norton, 1995).

Chapter VI

1. Geir Lundestad, *East, West, North, South: Major Developments in International Politics Since 1945*, 4th ed. (Oxford: Oxford University Press, 1999).

2. See Marc Trachtenberg, *A Constructed Peace: The Making of the European Settlement, 1945–1963* (Princeton: Princeton University Press, 1999).

3. Odd Arne Westad, Sven Holtsmark, and Iver B. Neumann, eds., *The Soviet Union in Eastern Europe, 1945–1989* (Basingstoke: Macmillan, 1994); Paul Dibb, *The Soviet Union: The Incomplete Superpower* (Urbana: University of Illinois Press, 1986).

4. Clark, *Globalization and Fragmentation*, pp. 137–40.

5. Geir Lundestad, *"Empire" by Integration: The United States and European Integration, 1945–1997* (Oxford: Oxford University Press, 1998).

6. See Alan S. Milward, *The European Rescue of the Nation-State* (Berkeley, Los Angeles, and London: University of California Press, 1992); Wilfried Loth, *Der Weg nach Europa. Geschichte der europäischen Integration 1939–1957*, 2d ed. (Göttingen: Vandenhoeck & Ruprecht, 1991).

7. See James N. Rosenau, *Turbulence in World Politics: A Theory of Change and Continuity* (London: Harvester Wheatsheaf, 1990).

8. David Held, Anthony McGrew, David Goldblatt, and Jonathan Perraton, *Global Transformations: Politics, Economics, and Culture* (Cambridge: Polity Press, 1999), p. 54.

9. Robert J. C. Young, *Postcolonialism: An Historical Introduction* (Oxford: Blackwell, 2001).

10. See Adam Roberts and Benedict Kingsbury, eds., *United Nations, Divided World: The UN's Roles in International Relations*, 2d ed. (Oxford: Clarendon Press, 1993).

11. Matthew Connelly, *A Diplomatic Revolution: Algeria's Fight for Independence and the Origins of the Post–Cold War Era* (Oxford: Oxford University Press, 2002).

12. Lewis, *Growth and Fluctuations*, p. 69.

13. Michael J. Hogan, *The Marshall Plan: America, Britain, and the Reconstruction of Western Europe, 1947–1952* (Cambridge: Cambridge University Press, 1987).

14. Geoffrey Jones, "Business Enterprises and Global Worlds," *Enterprise & Society* 3 (2002): 581–605.

15. Dunning, *Multinational Enterprises*; Mira Wilkins, *The Emergence of Multinational Enterprise: American Business Abroad from the Colonial Era to 1914* (Cambridge, Mass.: Harvard University Press,

1970); id., *The Maturing of Multinational Enterprise: American Business Abroad from 1914 to 1970* (Cambridge, Mass.: Harvard University Press, 1974).

16. Daniel Yergin, *The Prize: The Epic Quest for Oil, Money, and Power* (New York: Simon & Schuster, 1991).

17. Gary Gereffi and Donald L. Wyman, eds., *Manufacturing Miracles: Paths of Industrialization in Latin America and East Asia* (Princeton, N.J.: Princeton University Press, 1990).

18. Daniel Bell, *The End of Ideology: On the Exhaustion of Political Ideas in the Fifties*, 2d ed. (New York: Collier Books, 1961).

19. See Göran Therborn, *European Modernity and Beyond: The Trajectory of European Societies, 1945–2000* (London: Sage, 1995), pp. 47–50; Norman Naimark, *Fires of Hatred: Ethnic Cleansing in Twentieth-Century Europe* (Cambridge, Mass.: Harvard University Press, 2001).

20. Rob Kroes, *If You've Seen One, You've Seen the Mall: Europeans and American Mass Culture* (Urbana: University of Illinois Press, 1996).

21. See Uta G. Poiger, *Jazz, Rock, and Rebels: Cold War Politics and American Culture in a Divided Germany* (Berkeley, Los Angeles, and London: University of California Press, 2000).

22. See Saskia Sassen, *Cities in a World Economy* (Thousand Oaks, Calif.: Pine Forge Press, 1994).

23. See Hartmut Berghoff and Barbara Korte, eds., *The Making of Modern Tourism: The Cultural History of the British Experience, 1600–2000* (New York: Palgrave, 2002); Louis Turner and John Ash, *The Golden Hordes: International Tourism and the Pleasure Periphery* (London: Constable, 1975); A. G. Hopkins, "Globalization With and Without Empires: From Bali to Labrador," in *Globalization in World History*, ed. id., pp. 220–42.

24. James L. Watson, "Transnationalism, Localization, and Fast Food in East Asia," in *Golden Arches East: McDonald's in East Asia*, James L. Watson, ed. (Stanford: Stanford University Press, 1997), pp. 1–39, here p. 15.

25. Peter A. Hall and David Soskice, *Varieties of Capitalism: The Institutional Foundations of Comparative Advantage* (Oxford: Oxford University Press, 2001); Jonathan Zeitlin and Gary Herrigel, eds., *Americanization and Its Limits: Reworking U.S. Technology and Management in Post-war Europe and Japan* (Oxford: Oxford University Press, 2000).

26. See Carole Fink, Philipp Gassert, and Detlef Junker, eds., *1968: The World Transformed* (Cambridge: Cambridge University Press, 1998).

27. Arif Dirlik, "The Third World," in *1968*, eds. Fink et al., pp. 295–317.

28. John R. McNeill, *Something New Under the Sun: An Environmental History of the Twentieth-Century World* (New York: W. W. Norton, 2000), p. 51; Spencer R. Weart, *The Discovery of Global Warming* (Cambridge, Mass.: Harvard University Press, 2003), p. 39.

29. Donella H. Meadows et al., *The Limits to Growth: A Report for the Club of Rome's Project on the Predicament of Mankind* (New York: New American Library, 1972).

CHAPTER VII

1. See Manuel Castells, *The Internet Galaxy: Reflections on the Internet, Business, and Society* (Oxford: Blackwell, 2001), ch. 1.

2. See Yvonne Yazbeck Haddad, "The Globalization of Islam: The Return of Muslims to the West," in *The Oxford History of Islam*, John L. Esposito, ed. (Oxford: Oxford University Press, 1999), pp. 601–41.

3. For a description, see J. MacGaffey and R. Bazanguissa-Ganga, *Congo-Paris: Transnational Traders on the Margins of the Law* (Oxford: The International African Institute, 2000), p. 80.

4. Maurice Obstfeld and Alan M. Taylor, "International Capital Mobility in the Long Run," in *The Defining Moment: The Great Depression and the American Economy in the Twentieth Century*, Michael D. Bordo, Claudia D. Goldin, and Eugene N. White, eds. (Chicago and London: University of Chicago Press, 1998), pp. 353–403.

5. Karl Marx and Friedrich Engels, *The Communist Manifesto: A Modern Edition*, with an introduction by Eric J. Hobsbawm (London: Verso, 1998), p. 39.

6. "A New Workshop of the World," *The Economist*, 12 October 2002.

7. Impressively pictured in Le Monde Diplomatique, ed., *L'Atlas du Monde Diplomatique* (Paris: Le Monde Diplomatique, 2003).

8. Spyros Economides and Peter Wilson, *The Economic Factor in International Relations: A Brief Introduction* (London: Tauris, 2001), pp. 190–91.

9. See Albert O. Hirschman, *Exit, Voice, and Loyalty: Responses to Decline in Firms, Organizations, and States* (Cambridge: Cambridge University Press, 1970).

10. See S. N. Eisenstadt, "Multiple Modernities," *Daedalus* 129, no. 1 (2000): 1–30.

11. For a multifaceted economic analysis, see Jeffrey G. Williamson, *Winners and Losers Over Two Centuries of Globalization*, NBER Working Paper 9161, Cambridge, Mass., 2002.

Recommended Literature

THEORY AND METHODS: SOCIAL SCIENCES

Albrow, Martin. *The Global Age: State and Society Beyond Modernity.* Cambridge: Polity Press, 1996 [Stanford, Calif.: Stanford University Press, 1997].

Baylis, John, and Steve Smith, eds. *The Globalization of World Politics: An Introduction to International Relations.* 2d ed. Oxford: Oxford University Press, 2001.

Beck, Ulrich. *What Is Globalization?* Cambridge: Polity Press, 2000.

Ben-Rafael, Eliezer, and Yitzak Sternberg, eds. *Identity, Culture and Globalization.* Leiden: Brill, 2001.

Castells, Manuel. "Materials for an Exploratory Theory of the Network Society." *British Journal of Sociology* 51 (2000): 5–24.

———. *The Information Age: Economy, Society, and Culture.* 3 vols. 2d ed. Malden, Mass.: Blackwell, 2000–2004.

Giddens, Anthony. *The Consequences of Modernity.* Cambridge: Polity Press, 1991 [Stanford: Stanford University Press, 1990].

Held, David, Anthony McGrew, David Goldblatt, and Jonathan Perraton. *Global Transformations: Politics, Economics, and Culture.* Cambridge: Polity Press, 1999 [Stanford, Calif.: Stanford University Press, 1999].

Hirst, Paul, and Grahame Thompson. *Globalization in Question: The International Economy and the Possibilities of Governance.* 2d ed. Cambridge: Polity Press, 1999.

Michie, Jonathan, ed. *The Handbook of Globalisation.* Cheltenham: Edward Elgar, 2003.

Robertson, Roland. *Globalization: Social Theory and Global Culture.* London: Sage, 1992.

Robertson, Roland, and Kathleen E. White, eds. *Globalization: Critical Concepts in Sociology.* 6 vols. London and New York: Routledge, 2003.

Rosenau, James N. *Information Technologies and Global Politics: The Changing Scope of Power and Governance.* Albany: State University of New York Press, 2002.

Schirato, Tony, and Jen Webb, eds. *Understanding Globalization.* London: Sage, 2003.

Scholte, Jan A. *Globalization: A Critical Introduction.* Basingstoke and New York: Palgrave, 2000.

THEORY AND METHODS: WORLD HISTORY

Adas, Michael, ed. *Islamic and European Expansion: The Forging of a Global Order.* Philadelphia, Penn.: Temple University Press, 1993.

Bairoch, Paul. *Economics and World History: Myths and Paradoxes.* New York: Harvester Wheatsheaf, 1993.

Bender, Thomas, ed. *Rethinking American History in a Global Age.* Berkeley, Los Angeles, and London: University of California Press, 2002.

Cooper, Frederick. "What Is the Concept of Globalization Good For? An African Historian's Perspective." *African Affairs* 100 (2001): 189–213.

Dunn, Ross E., ed. *The New World History: A Teacher's Companion.* Boston: Bedford/St. Martin's, 2000.

Geyer, Michael, and Charles Bright. "World History in a Global Age." *American Historical Review* 100 (1995): 1034–60.

Hopkins, A. G., ed. *Globalization in World History.* London: Pimlico, 2002.

Manning, Patrick. *Navigating World History: Historians Create a Global Past.* New York: Palgrave, 2003.

Maier, Charles S. "Consigning the Twentieth Century to History: Alternative Narratives for the Modern Era." *American Historical Review* 105 (2000): 807–31.

Mazlish, Bruce, and Ralph Buultjens, eds. *Conceptualizing Global History.* Boulder, Colo.: Westview Press, 1993.

Osterhammel, Jürgen. *Geschichtswissenschaft jenseits des National-staats. Studien zu Beziehungsgeschichte und Zivilisationsvergleich.* Göttingen: Vandenhoeck & Ruprecht, 2001.

Pomper, Philip, Richard H. Elphick, and Richard T. Vann, eds. *World History: Ideologies, Structures, and Identities.* Oxford: Blackwell, 1998.

Stuchtey, Benedikt, and Eckhardt Fuchs, eds. *Writing World History, 1800–2000*. Oxford: Oxford University Press, 2003.

THE VERY BIG PICTURE: GLOBAL AND WORLD HISTORY

Arrighi, Giovanni. *The Long Twentieth Century: Money, Power, and the Origins of Our Times*. London and New York: Verso, 1994.
Bulliet, Richard W., Pamela Kyle Crossley, Daniel R. Headrick, Steven W. Hirsch, Lyman L. Johnson, and David Northrup, eds. *The Earth and Its Peoples: A Global History*. 2d ed. Boston and New York: Houghton Mifflin, 2001.
Christian, David. *Maps of Time: An Introduction to Big History*. Berkeley: University of California Press, 2004.
Fernández-Armesto, Felipe. *Millennium*. London: Bantam, 1995.
Goody, Jack. *Capitalism and Modernity: The Great Debate*. Cambridge: Polity Press, 2004.
Howard, Michael, and Wm. Roger Louis, eds. *The Oxford History of the Twentieth Century*. Oxford: Oxford University Press, 1998.
McNeill, William H., and John R. McNeill. *The Human Web: A Bird's-Eye View of World History*. New York: W. W. Norton, 2003.
Pomeranz, Kenneth. *The Great Divergence: China, Europe, and the Making of the Modern World Economy*. Princeton, N.J.: Princeton University Press, 2000.
Stearns, Peter N., Michael Adas, and Stuart B. Schwartz. *World Civilizations: The Global Experience*. 2 vols. 2d ed. New York: HarperCollins, 1996.
Tignor, Robert L., Jeremy Adelman, Stephen Aron, Gyan Prakash, Stephen Kotkin, Suzanne Marchand, and Michael Tsin. *Worlds Together, Worlds Apart: A History of the Modern World (1300 to the Present)*. New York: W. W. Norton, 2002.

THE BIG PICTURE: SPECIFIC PERIODS IN OVERVIEW

Abu-Lughod, Janet. *Before European Hegemony: The World System, A.D. 1250–1350*. New York and Oxford: Oxford University Press, 1989.

Bayly, C. A. *The Birth of the Modern World, 1780–1914*. Oxford: Blackwell, 2004.

Curtin, Philip D. *The World and the West: European Challenge and the Overseas Response in the Age of Empire*. Cambridge: Cambridge University Press, 2000.

Gunn, Geoffrey C. *First Globalization: The Eurasian Exchange, 1500–1800*. Lanham, Md.: Rowman & Littlefield, 2003.

Hobsbawm, Eric. *The Age of Empire, 1875–1914*. London: Cardinal, 1989 [New York: Pantheon Books, 1987; Vintage, 1989].

———. *The Age of Extremes: A History of the World, 1914–1991*. New York: Pantheon Books, 1995.

Nussbaum, Felicity A., ed. *The Global Eighteenth Century*. Baltimore: Johns Hopkins University Press, 2003.

Reynolds, David. *One World Divisible: A Global History Since 1945*. New York: W. W. Norton, 2000.

Roberts, John M. *Twentieth Century: The History of the World, 1901 to 2000*. New York: Penguin, 1999.

Strachan, Hew. *The First World War*. Vol. 1: *To Arms*. Oxford: Oxford University Press, 2001.

Weinberg, Gerald L. *A World at Arms: A Global History of World War II*. Cambridge: Cambridge University Press, 1994.

Wills, John E., Jr. *1688: A Global History*. New York and London: W. W. Norton, 2001.

MACROREGIONS

Armitage, David, and Michael J. Braddick, eds. *The British Atlantic World, 1500–1800*. Basingstoke: Palgrave, 2002.

Barendse, R. J. *The Arabian Seas: The Indian Ocean World of the Seventeenth Century*. Armonk and London: Sharpe, 2002.

Chaudhuri, K. N. *Trade and Civilisation in the Indian Ocean: An Economic History from the Rise of Islam to 1750*. Cambridge: Cambridge University Press, 1985.

———. *Asia Before Europe: Economy and Civilization of the Indian Ocean from the Rise of Islam to 1750*. Cambridge: Cambridge University Press, 1990.

Curtin, Philip D. *The Rise and Fall of the Plantation Complex*. Cambridge: Cambridge University Press, 1990.

Flynn, Dennis O., Lionel Frost, and A. J. H. Latham, eds. *Pacific Centuries: Pacific and Pacific Rim History Since the Sixteenth Century*. London and New York: Routledge, 1999.

Gruzinski, Serge. *Les quatre parties du monde: Histoire d'une mondialisation*. Paris: Éditions de La Martinière, 2004.

Jones, Eric L., Lionel Frost, and Colin White. *Coming Full Circle: An Economic History of the Pacific Rim*. Boulder, Colo.: Westview Press, 1993.

Lieberman, Victor, ed. *Beyond Binary Histories: Re-imagining Eurasia to c. 1830*. Ann Arbor: University of Michigan Press, 1999.

Pietschman, Horst, ed. *Atlantic History: History of the Atlantic System, 1580–1830*. Göttingen: Vandenhoeck & Ruprecht, 2002.

Russell-Wood, A. J. R. *The Portuguese Empire, 1415–1808: A World on the Move*. Baltimore: Johns Hopkins University Press, 1998.

Stein, Stanley J., and Barbara Stein. *Silver, Trade, and War: Spain and America in the Making of Early Modern Europe*. Baltimore: Johns Hopkins University Press, 2000.

Thornton, John K. *Africa and Africans in the Making of the Atlantic World, 1450–1800*. 2d ed. Cambridge: Cambridge University Press, 1998.

International Relations, Empires, and Imperialism

Abernethy, David B. *The Dynamics of Global Dominance: European Overseas Empires, 1415–1980*. New Haven and London: Yale University Press, 2000.

Bull, Hedley, and Adam Watson, eds. *The Expansion of International Society*. Oxford: Clarendon Press, 1984.

Buzan, Barry, and Richard Little. *International Systems in World History: Remaking the Study of International Relations*. Oxford: Oxford University Press, 2000.

Clark, Ian. *Globalization and Fragmentation: International Relations in the Twentieth Century*. Oxford: Oxford University Press, 1997.

Doyle, Michael W. *Empires*. Ithaca and London: Cornell University Press, 1986.

Eckes, Alfred E., and Thomas W. Zeiler. *Globalization and the American Century*. Cambridge: Cambridge University Press, 2003.

Geyer, Martin H., and Johannes Paulmann, eds. *The Mechanics of Internationalism: Culture, Society, and Politics from the 1840s to the First World War*. Oxford: Oxford University Press, 2001.

Girault, René. *Diplomatie européenne et impérialismes: Histoire des relations internationales contemporaines*. Vol. 1: *1871–1914*. Paris: Masson, 1979.

Girault, René, and Robert Frank. *Turbulente Europe et nouveaux mondes: Histoire des relations internationales contemporaines*. Vol. 2: *1914–1941*. Paris: Masson, 1988.

Holland, Robert F. *European Decolonization, 1918–1981*. Basingstoke: Macmillan, 1985.

Iriye, Akira. *The Globalizing of America, 1913–1945*. Cambridge: Cambridge University Press, 1993.

Kennedy, Paul M. *The Rise and Fall of the Great Powers: Economic Change and Military Conflict from 1500 to 2000*. London: Unwin Hyman, 1988.

Keylor, William R. *The Twentieth-Century World: An International History*. 4th ed. New York: Oxford University Press, 2001.

———. *A World of Nations: The International Order Since 1945*. New York: Oxford University Press, 2003.

Lieven, Dominic. *Empire: The Russian Empire and Its Rivals*. London: Murray, 2000.

Lundestad, Geir. *East, West, North, South: Major Developments in International Politics Since 1945*. 4th ed. Oxford: Oxford University Press, 1999.

Motyl, Alexander J. *Imperial Ends: The Decay, Collapse, and Revival of Empires*. New York: Columbia University Press, 2001.

Ninkovich, Frank. *The Wilsonian Century: U.S. Foreign Policy Since 1900*. Chicago and London: University of Chicago Press, 1999.

Osiander, Andreas. *The States System of Europe, 1640–1990: Peacemaking and the Conditions of International Stability*. Oxford: Clarendon Press, 1994.

Osterhammel, Jürgen. *Colonialism: A Theoretical Overview*. 2d ed. Princeton, N. J.: Markus Wiener, 2005.

Rosenberg, Emily. *Spreading the American Dream: American Economic and Cultural Diplomacy, 1890–1945*. New York: Hill & Wang, 1982.

Wesseling, Henk L. *The European Colonial Empires*. Harlow: Longman, 2004.

Young, John W. *The Longman Companion to America, Russia, and the Cold War, 1941–1998*. 2d ed. London: Longman, 1999.

The World Economy

Beckert, Sven. *The Empire of Cotton: A Global History*. New York: Knopf (forthcoming).

Bordo, Michael D., Alan M. Taylor, and Jeffrey G. Williamson, eds. *Globalization in Historical Perspective*. Chicago: University of Chicago Press, 2003.

Cameron, Rondo. *A Concise Economic History of the World: From Paleolithic Times to the Present*. 2 vols. 4th ed. New York: Oxford University Press, 2003.

Curtin, Philip D. *Cross-Cultural Trade in World History*. Cambridge: Cambridge University Press, 1984.

Davis, Ralph. *The Rise of the Atlantic Economies*. London: Weidenfeld & Nicolson, 1973 [Ithaca, N.Y.: Cornell University Press, 1973].

Dunning, John H. *Multinational Enterprises and the Global Economy*. Wokingham: Addison-Wesley, 1993.

Fischer, Wolfram. *Expansion, Integration, Globalisierung. Studien zur Geschichte der Weltwirtschaft*. Göttingen: Vandenhoeck & Ruprecht, 1998.

Fischer, Wolfram, R. Marvin McInnis, and Jürgen Schneider, eds. *The Emergence of a World Economy*. 2 vols. Wiesbaden: Steiner, 1986.

Harms, Bernhard. *Volkswirtschaft und Weltwirtschaft. Versuch der Begründung einer Weltwirtschaftslehre*. Jena: Fischer Verlag, 1912.

Hugill, Peter J. *World Trade Since 1431: Geography, Technology, and Capitalism*. Baltimore: Johns Hopkins University Press, 1993.

———. *Global Communications Since 1844: Geopolitics and Technology*. Baltimore and London: Johns Hopkins University Press, 1999.

Inikori, Joseph E. *Africans and the Industrial Revolution in England: A Study in International Trade and Economic Development*. Cambridge: Cambridge University Press, 2002.

James, Harold. *The End of Globalization: Lessons from the Great Depression*. Cambridge, Mass.: Harvard University Press, 2001.

Kenwood, Albert G., and Alan L. Lougheed. *The Growth of the International Economy, 1820–2000: An Introductory Text.* 4th ed. London: Routledge, 1999.

O'Rourke, Kevin H., and Jeffrey G. Williamson. *Globalization and History: The Evolution of a Nineteenth-Century Atlantic Economy.* Cambridge, Mass.: MIT Press, 1999.

Rothermund, Dietmar. *The Global Impact of the Great Depression, 1929–1939.* London and New York: Routledge, 1996.

Tracy, James D., ed. *The Rise of Merchant Empires: Long-Distance Trade in the Early Modern World, 1350–1750.* Cambridge: Cambridge University Press, 1990.

———. *The Political Economy of Merchant Empires.* Cambridge: Cambridge University Press, 1991.

Yergin, Daniel. *The Prize: The Epic Quest for Oil, Money, and Power.* New York: Simon & Schuster, 1991.

Voluntary and Involuntary Migration

Bade, Klaus J. *Migration in European History.* Oxford: Blackwell, 2003.

Eltis, David, ed. *Coerced and Free Migration: Global Perspectives.* Stanford, Calif.: Stanford University Press, 2002.

Hoerder, Dirk. *Cultures in Contact: World Migration in the Second Millennium.* Durham, N.C.: Duke University Press, 2002.

Klein, Herbert S. *The Atlantic Slave Trade.* Cambridge: Cambridge University Press, 1999.

Solow, Barbara L., ed. *Slavery and the Rise of the Atlantic System.* Cambridge: Cambridge University Press, 1988.

Wang, Gungwu, ed. *Global History and Migrations.* Boulder, Colo.: Westview Press, 1997.

Environmental History

Crosby, Alfred W. *Ecological Imperialism: The Biological Expansion of Europe, 900–1900.* Cambridge: Cambridge University Press, 1986.

McNeill, John R. *Something New Under the Sun: An Environmental History of the Twentieth-Century World.* New York and London: W. W. Norton, 2000.

McNeill, William H. *Plagues and Peoples*. Harmondsworth: Penguin, 1976.

Richards, John F. *The Unending Frontier: An Environmental History of the Early Modern World*. Berkeley, Los Angeles, and London: University of California Press, 2003.

KNOWLEDGE, IDEOLOGY, AND CULTURE

Briggs, Asa, and Peter Burke. *A Social History of the Media: From Gutenberg to the Internet*. Cambridge: Polity Press, 2002.

Crystal, David. *English as a Global Language*. 2d ed. Cambridge: Cambridge University Press, 2003.

Greenhalgh, Paul. *Ephemeral Vistas: The Expositions Universelles, Great Exhibitions, and World's Fairs, 1851–1939*. Manchester: Manchester University Press, 1988.

Hastings, Adrian, ed. *A World History of Christianity*. London: Cassell, 1999.

Headrick, Daniel R. *The Invisible Weapon: Telecommunications and International Politics, 1851–1945*. New York: Oxford University Press, 1988.

———. *The Tentacles of Progress: Technology Transfer in the Age of Imperialism, 1850–1940*. New York: Oxford University Press, 1988.

Kroes, Rob. *If You've Seen One, You've Seen the Mall: Europeans and American Mass Culture*. Urbana: University of Illinois Press, 1996.

Trumpbour, John. *Selling Hollywood to the World: United States and European Struggles for Mastery of the Global Film Industry, 1920–1950*. Cambridge: Cambridge University Press, 2002.

Voll, John Obert. *Islam: Continuity and Change in the Modern World*. Boulder, Colo.: Westview Press, 1982.

Index

capital markets, capital flow, 15, 62, 85, 86, 104–6, 126, 128, 142

civilizations, 4, 14, 19–21, 32, 34, 36, 46, 48, 50f., 58, 66, 72f., 104, 133, 136, 150f.

colonies, 18, 49, 51–54, 59, 60, 70–73, 78, 87, 92, 98, 100, 132

communication, 2, 7–9, 14, 22, 24, 28, 34, 46, 69, 80, 86, 90, 92, 97, 126, 128, 144, 146, 151

consumption, 2, 23, 52, 79, 108, 123, 131–35, 138, 144

culture, 7, 27, 36, 46, 52, 54, 56, 75f., 108, 113, 131, 132, 138, 142, 150

decolonialization, 119, 132

deglobalization, fragmentation, 10, 26, 29, 36, 40, 81, 95, 127, 150

diaspora, 16, 145, 150

distance, space, 6, 8, 16, 26, 38, 82–84, 90f., 106, 113, 149f.

empire, 18, 28, 32, 36–38, 40–44, 60, 69–71, 90, 92, 99, 106, 117–19

environment, 9, 19, 24, 29, 138f., 142

epidemics, 45, 98, 152

experience, globalization experience, 2f., 16, 77, 81f., 111, 117, 133, 146

free trade, 6, 28, 57–80, 92, 99

globalization (term, definition), 1–13, 14, 21–27, 130–52

globalization thrusts, 27, 35, 57

ideologies, 3f., 69f., 100f., 115, 118, 128, 130f., 141–43

imperialism, 17–19, 46, 70, 92, 137, 146

industry, Industrial Revolution, 28, 51, 57, 60, 62–69, 76, 93f., 104, 108, 110f., 135

institutions, 10, 15f., 23, 26, 28, 45, 63, 65, 71–73, 86, 119, 122f., 135

integration, connections, 25–29, 30, 32, 34f., 37, 40, 48–50, 61, 64, 70, 79, 81, 84, 86–90, 106, 113–20, 145, 150

interaction sphere, 24, 25

international organizations, 95–97, 99f., 103, 120–24, 129, 142

international system, 90–95, 99–102, 114–18, 141

language, 1, 45, 52, 76, 145

markets, 2, 6, 9, 16, 63, 69, 70, 79, 85, 90, 94, 104, 118, 127f., 143f., 147

media, 7, 75f., 82, 131–33, 137, 144

migration, immigration and emigration, 14–16, 25, 34f., 48, 77f., 89, 131f., 148, 150

military, weaponry, 10, 17, 26f., 32, 35–37, 40, 44, 58–60, 65, 66, 70, 72, 92, 95–97, 101, 114f., 119, 124, 131, 150

modernity, modernization, 4, 5, 60, 72, 100f., 111, 122, 130, 133f., 136, 150f.

money, currency, 11, 22, 86, 88f., 98, 104–6, 122–27, 131

nation-state, 6, 7, 14, 17, 20, 24, 28, 74, 86, 90, 99, 116–21, 130, 146, 148, 150
network, 8f., 21–26, 28, 32, 43f., 49, 66, 75, 79, 80, 87, 92, 97, 128, 142–50

region, regionalism, 35f., 39–41, 47–50, 60, 65, 68, 76, 78f., 85–88, 94, 97, 106f., 110, 123, 133, 135, 147f.
religions, 32–34, 53, 73, 75

science and knowledge, 52, 54, 74, 84
slavery, slave trade, 16, 24, 48, 73, 77, 145, 146
state, 6, 8, 41, 57f., 60, 69f., 88–90, 95, 99f., 102, 105, 117–19, 125–28, 136, 142

technology, 7, 9, 23, 25, 44, 46, 66, 79, 101, 109, 143, 144, 151
time, 6, 8, 67, 69, 77, 82f.

trade, 14–16, 24, 28, 34, 48–50, 53, 66f., 68f., 85f., 97, 104–6, 122–25, 129, 142, 145, 148
transportation, 57f., 65–69, 86, 90, 146, 150
travel, tourism, 7, 52, 68, 133

universalization, 7, 74, 102

war, 38f., 41, 47f., 58–60, 65, 70, 75, 92, 94, 95, 97f., 102, 118f., 131, 136f., 141
Westernization, Americanization, 26, 108, 132, 136, 138, 144, 149
world economy, global economy, 3, 14, 20–22, 28f., 61, 65, 70, 76f., 79, 81–89, 92, 103–8, 116, 119, 121f., 127–33, 141, 145
world politics, 29, 59, 81, 92–95, 99, 107f., 119, 141f.
world system, 20f., 31
world war, 17, 29, 81–84, 97, 101–3, 107–11, 117, 121f.